June 1989

Dear Andrew,

I hope you
enjoy this. We will
miss you in Primary.
Continue to grow and
serve all the days of
your life. Remember
always, the simple
teachings of your
Primary teachers they
will sustain you in
all you do in your
life.

Love,

Sister Preston

If Talent Were Pizza, You'd Be a Supreme

Introduction

You probably know me as the author of the novel *Charly*.

It was as much a surprise to me as anyone else to find out I'd written a best-seller. The truth is that I have very little training to be a writer—most of my education has been in math and physics.

Once, as a graduate student in physics, I signed up for a course in creative writing. One day I told the teacher I wanted to be a published writer of fiction. He raised his eyebrows, probably recalling the string of *C* grades I'd received so far in the class, and asked, "You're not serious, are you?"

What could I say? Here was a highly educated professional who didn't believe I had what it takes. And of course he was right—I didn't show much promise as a writer then. But there's one thing he couldn't measure. He couldn't know how strong my desire to write was. In fact at the time I didn't know how strong it was either.

Eventually I dropped the course, telling myself that I'd tried and that's all a person could do. I was willing to let that dream snuff out. But it wouldn't snuff. It just lay there and smoldered.

A few years later I got enough courage to try it again. I signed up for a correspondence course in writing. The course cost me $37.50. Besides that, I had to rent a type-writer too. I felt bad about splurging on myself, so I decided to send a story to the *New Era* magazine and see if they would accept it. If they did, it would at least help pay for part of my expenses.

To my surprise they accepted my story. Not only that but Brian Kelly, the editor, seemed genuinely enthusiastic about my writing. Since then I've written over twenty stories for the *New Era*. Brian Kelly has been important in my life because he was the first person to encourage me to continue writing.

In May of 1979 I set a goal to write a novel. I still have my journal entry for that day: "I will write a novel and send it off to a publisher by October. That is my goal. I will do it whether or not it's ever published."

Charly's first printing was sold out in three weeks. It has since sold over one hundred thousand copies. Since *Charly*, I have written six other novels.

The reason for telling you this is so you'll understand that it could've gone either way for me—I might've just as easily given up.

I've been thinking about you lately, about your talents, especially the ones you don't know about yet. There's something I've got to tell you before you do what I almost did, before you give up on yourself, before you let your dreams die out, before you choose to be less than God wants you to be.

I want you to understand that I believe no matter who you are, *God has given you great talents*.

Maybe you don't know what they are yet, or maybe you only know one or two of them, but there's a bunch of them there all right. It's like the sweepstakes letter that begins "You May Already Be A Winner," except when it comes to talents, *you already are a winner*. Since your existence didn't begin at birth, you came to the earth already laden with talents, and all you have to do is find out what they are.

If talent were pizza, you'd be a supreme with extra cheese. If talent were water, you'd be the Atlantic Ocean. If talent were a car, you'd be a Corvette. That's true not only of you, but everyone else also. Unfortunately some people have been led into thinking they aren't very talented. That's a tragedy; it's like using a twenty-pound diamond as a doorstop.

I hope this book will help you discover the storehouse of talent that lies within you.

CHAPTER ONE

You Were Also in the Beginning

After your earth life one of the things the Lord will want to know is "what you personally have done with the talents you were given in the preexistence." (President David O. McKay.)

How old are you?

Nope, sorry, you're wrong. Actually you're thousands of years old. "Man was also in the beginning with God. Intelligence, or the light of truth, was not created or made, neither indeed can be." (D&C 93:29.)

You also were in the beginning with God before the earth was formed. That means you've been around for a long time. How long? Try forever.

Since infinity is a tough concept, let's pick a number that seems plenty big. How about ten thousand years? For the purposes of this discussion then, before you were born, you existed for ten thousand years in our premortal existence.

What did you do for those ten thousand years before you came to earth? You must have done something. As far as we know, there was no trash to take out, lawns to mow, dishes to wash, or weeds to pull. Would you like me to explain what you did for the thousands of years before you were born?

Okay, I admit it, I can't. My memory about our life before coming to earth is as bad as yours. But I have a theory. I think we kept busy. Maybe some of us were in a choir or orchestra, or else fixed cars or stars or whatever needed fixing. A few of us wrote songs. Maybe the future psychologists among us went around asking people how they were feeling. Others might have been interested in learning exactly what makes a star shine. Maybe some of us even gave some suggestions for the design of the mosquito. (If that was you, I've got a serious complaint.)

Read carefully what President Joseph F. Smith said: "Our spirits existed before they came to this world. They were in the councils of the heavens before the foundations of the earth were laid. We were there. We sang together with the heavenly hosts for joy when the foundations of the earth were laid, and when the plan of our existence upon this earth and redemption were mapped out. We were there; we were interested, and we took a part in this great preparation."

Did you catch the fact that we sang together? So we were in a choir after all! I wonder which of us wrote the music we sang. Bach or Mozart? Or maybe even you.

Whatever it was we did before coming to earth, we probably got good at it. It must have been to our advantage to have all that time. Suppose you spent an hour a day for ten thousand years practicing the piano, how good at it could you get? Plenty good, right? Even your piano teacher would notice the improvement.

Another advantage of our pre-earth life is that we spent it with our Heavenly Father. President Joseph Fielding Smith said: "There was a time before we ever came into this world when we dwelt in God's presence. We knew what kind of a being he is. One thing we saw was how glorious he is. Another thing, how great was his wisdom, his understanding, how wonderful was his power and his inspiration. And we wanted to be like him."

We also knew that Heavenly Father loved us. What would it be like to have someone as wonderful as God tell you that he loves you? How could anyone feel unimportant after that?

I think it's important to realize that Heavenly Father is very creative and talented, and because we're his children, we've naturally inherited some of that. I'm sure he loves to see us take after him. I would like to believe that before we came to earth we brought him our scraps of poetry, our songs, and our mathematical equations. We showed them to him in sort of a premortal show-and-tell. I believe he loved it all, not because it was that good, but because it showed that we were developing our own talents. Our Father in Heaven encouraged us to learn, to grow, and to develop.

As every high school senior knows, there's just so much growth you can have while living with your parents. After a while it's time to move on, to get away, to see if you can live the right way on your own. I believe that's one reason we had to come to earth. We had to prove we could live righteously even though we weren't living in our Heavenly Father's presence. We also needed to get a genuine physical body.

When the game plan about earth life was explained to us, we must have been really excited. It was probably like being selected to play in the Super Bowl. The scriptures say that when we heard the plan, we shouted for joy. I can't tell you the exact words we were shouting, but I think we said something like this: "All right! We'll be true and faithful! We'll use our talents for good! Father, we're going to make you proud of us!"

And so this earth life was to be our big chance to prove ourselves. Here's what President Joseph Fielding Smith said: "If we will just be true and faithful to every covenant, to every principle of truth that he has given us, then after the resurrection we would come back into his presence and we would be just like he is. We would have the same kind of bodies—bodies that would shine like the sun."

I'm sure we were anxious to go to the earth, but for us it must have seemed to take forever. Generations passed by while we waited. We were like an eager quarterback watching from the sidelines, wanting to get in the game.

Our time to be born had been carefully selected. It would be when the fullness of the gospel was on the earth, close to the Second Coming, when there was a need for those who had proven themselves to be valiant in their premortal existence.

President Harold B. Lee said: "Who are you? You are all sons and daughters of God. Your spirits were created and lived as organized intelligences before the world was. You have been blessed to have a physical body because of your obedience to certain commandments in that pre-mortal state. You are now born into a family to which you have come, into the nations through which you have come, as a reward for the kind of lives you lived before you came here."

Then, after another several thousand years, it finally happened. Your spirit entered the body of a baby, and shortly after, you were born. At first it must have seemed very strange to have a physical body. It was probably like trying to learn how to run a complicated piece of machinery without an instruction manual. Just learning how to pick up a toy took weeks. After a while, before we could tell anybody on earth, we forgot all about our life with our Heavenly Father.

For the first few years of our earth life, we were adored. The first time we said "Dada" or "Mama" or even "gaga," we were showered with love and affection. It was really great. We were the center of our parents' lives. Each step along the way was greeted with praise and adoration. The first time we talked, walked, or became potty-trained; the day our parents could leave us in the nursery at church without us crying; our first day of kindergarten. In some ways it was a lot like before we came to earth. We were learning new skills, and we were being praised, adored, and comforted when we were in need.

Then came that eventful day we started school. Kindergarten was okay. We had naps and milk and graham crackers, and the teacher put everyone's artwork on the bulletin board for everyone to see. As we progressed through school, however, things gradually changed. I remember the first time I realized that my teacher hadn't put my crayon drawing on the wall. It didn't seem fair. It should have been up there because it was the best I could do. It was the first time I realized that maybe my best wasn't good enough.

The S's for satisfactory in grade school sometimes turn to C's for average in junior high. I remember the awful feeling I had when I first realized that maybe I wasn't special after all.

Bit by bit, year by year, if we're not careful, this earth life can take away the confidence we had while we lived in the preexistence. To make matters worse, eventually we reach adolescence. Suddenly our face breaks out, our voice cracks, our hair looks like straw, and we start stumbling in front of large groups of people. Our parents tell us we're too young for some things and, a minute later, lecture to us that we're too old for other things. People ask what we want to be when we grow up, and somehow they're not as thrilled with the old answers. We know they expect more than a simple answer like we want to be a fireman or a jet pilot or She-ra, Princess of Power.

About this time in our lives, peer pressure calls the

shots. If we're not careful, we can spend the greater portion of our teenage years trying to be exactly like our friends. We will do anything to avoid looking ridiculous to our peers. If some friends ask us to go play golf with them, we'll sometimes refuse because we don't know how to play golf and we don't want to make fools of ourselves in front of everyone. We don't play tennis because we don't know how to play tennis. We don't take algebra because we heard it was hard. We stand around on the sidelines at dances because we don't know how to dance and we're afraid of looking dumb if we try.

And so we go about building our own prisons, voluntarily limiting ourselves. If we're not careful, we may never break out. That would be a great tragedy, because it means that your unique gift to give mankind might never be given.

People seldom go beyond their self-imposed barriers. People who say "I can't do it" hardly ever do. People who say "I'm clumsy" often stay away from physical activity. Those who think to themselves "I'm ugly" may never discover their attractive features. People who say "I'm dumb" may avoid learning how to use their minds. This is so foreign to what Heavenly Father wants for us. If only we could feel once again the way we felt when we were living with him. If only we could listen to his encouraging words about our own infinite possibilities.

We all, at some time in our life, need to break out of our self-imposed prison and tear off the negative labels we've carried around with us. We need to become the positive, energetic, hopeful, dynamic person God meant us to be. Perhaps it's that time for you. Instead of being paralyzed by your past, you need to plan for your future.

"Now the Lord had shown unto me, Abraham, the intelligences that were organized before the world was; and among all these there were many of the noble and great ones; and God saw these souls that they were good, and he stood in the midst of them, . . . and he said unto me: Abraham, thou art one of them; thou wast chosen before thou wast born." (Abraham 3: 22-23.)

Believe it or not, you were also among the noble and great ones that were organized before the world was. Just as God said it to Abraham, he could have also said it to you: Barb, Dan, Brad, Jed, Josie, Rachel, Gay, Ben, Wendy, Seth, Sarah, Allyson, Kate, Jennifer, Matthew, Jason, Amanda, David, Ryan, James, Heather, Joshua, Melissa, Michael, Nicole, John, Kelly, Daniel, Jessica, Steven, Michelle, Brian, Alicia, Timothy, Elizabeth, Eric, Rebecca, Jeff, Kimberly, Nick, Amy, Adam, Cadi, Charlotte, Laurie, Sean, Emily, William . . . (Did I leave anybody out? Sorry about that. Do me a favor and pencil in your name. Go ahead, I've left you some room.) . . . Justin, Jan, Jared, Tara, Sterling, Tassa, Travis, Melinda, Jeremy, Lindsay, Holly, Kristin, Carl, Libby, Matt, _____, "thou art one of them; thou wast chosen before thou wast born."

CHAPTER TWO

Peanut Butter on the Hook

A week later I took Charly fishing at Strawberry Reservoir. We left at four A.M. When we arrived, I rented a boat, rowed to my favorite spot, threw out both anchors, and started to fish.

She curled up in an old army blanket and went to sleep.

By the time she woke up, I had caught four nice trout, the sun had come and driven off the patches of fog from the lake, and ten other boats had joined us.

She studied the people in the boats near us, who were all quietly watching their lines.

Suddenly she stood up, cleared her throat, and with a Kissinger-like accent addressed the other boaters: "I suppose you know why we've asked you all here this morning. If it meets with your approval, we'll dispense with the minutes and proceed."

The boaters glanced at her with disbelief.

"Because some of you have been putting marshmallows on your hooks, the Utah Fish and Game Department, hereafter referred to as the UFGD, has asked me to speak today. Clinical reports just released indicate that the fish in this lake have fifty-three percent more cavities."

She paused and then yelled sharply, "DO YOU KNOW WHAT THIS MEANS?"

She waited for an answer but nobody spoke. Most tried to ignore her, but that was hard to do.

"It means the UFGD must now stand the expense of sending a trout through dental school!"

"Charly?" I said.

"Yes, Utah," she answered demurely.

"Normally we don't talk between boats."

"So?"

"So sit down and be quiet."

She sat down. I baited her hook and threw it out. In a few minutes, her line began to feed out smoothly and steadily. When she set the hook, I could tell it was going to be big. Screaming and giggling, doing an impersonation of Captain Ahab after Moby Dick, she reeled in the line and soon I dipped the net into the water and brought up a four-pound trout.

After I had taken care of the fish, she stood up again. "Do you want to know how I caught this fish? I used peanut butter on the hook. It sticks well, and it does not, does not, I repeat—cause little fish cavities."

Quickly I pulled in both anchors and began to row away.

"We recommend creamy instead of chunky!" she yelled as her parting shot. (From the novel *Charly*.)

For as long as I can remember I've always known I was a good fisherman. Let me give you an example. One day I decided to go fishing at a lake. By the time I arrived, there were already several people lined up on the bank near where I usually fished. I realized after I got there that I'd forgotten any bait, so I asked a nearby fisherman if I could borrow a worm. Within half an hour I'd caught my limit on that one worm while several of those around me hadn't caught anything. For some reason I was in a hurry and had to leave. "Thanks for the worm," I said as I passed the one who'd loaned it to me.

Do you see what I mean? I'm magic when it comes to fishing.

When I catch a lot of fish, I think, "Well, sure I did okay. That's because I'm a good fisherman." When I don't catch anything, I think, "Hey, if I didn't have any luck then nobody else did either, because I'm a good fisherman. Maybe it's the full moon or the rain last night or it's too hot or . . ." Whatever happens, I always interpret it in terms of my unshakable belief that I'm a good fisherman.

A couple of years ago I started wondering why I've always had this self-confidence about fishing. I think that I've finally figured it out.

When I was boy, living in Montana, my parents used to take me fishing. We would rent a boat and go trolling. Every time we went, my dad would bait my hook first, throw it overboard, then bait my mother's hook, and finally his own. Because my hook was in the water as much as ten minutes before anybody else's, I often caught the first fish.

When I reeled in the first catch of the day, my dad would say, "Jack always catches the first fish. That's because he's a good fisherman."

I believed my dad.

He could have told me the truth. He could have said, "Hey, kid, don't let it go to your head. The only reason you caught the first fish is because your line was in the water before anybody else's." But he didn't. Both my parents kept reassuring me that I was a good fisherman. Within a few years it became one of those rock-solid beliefs that nothing can shake.

When I was in the sixth grade, our family moved to another part of the state. After that I didn't go fishing much. In fact I didn't fish again until after my mission, while I was a graduate student at BYU. The first place I fished was at Strawberry Reservoir in Utah. (That's where the idea for the fishing scene from *Charly* came from.)

When I started fishing again, what did I know about fishing? Not a thing. When I was a kid and went with my dad, he tied the knots, baited the hook, and knew where to go to catch fish and how deep to troll. My dad did it all. All I did was reel.

And yet there I was, every Saturday in the summer, sitting in a boat at Strawberry Reservoir, knowing full well I was going to catch a lot of fish.

When I did manage to catch fish, it reinforced my belief that I was a good fisherman. And when I didn't, I figured the fish just weren't biting that day.

I hope you're beginning to see that this chapter isn't really about fishing. The point is that because I had this unshakable faith that I was a good fisherman, I never gave up. And because I didn't give up, I eventually learned the skills that turned me into what I had always believed I was in the first place—a good fisherman. The self-confidence came first and then came the skills to back it up.

Now take the opposite case. What if someone believes that he's terrible at fishing? If he goes fishing and doesn't catch anything, he thinks, "I never catch any fish. That's because I'm no good at fishing." If he does catch a fish, what does he think? "It doesn't make any difference. I'm still no good at fishing."

You either catch fish or you don't. But you will always interpret what happens in terms of what you believe about yourself as a fisherman.

If you believe you're good at fishing, you'll keep going until you become good at it. If you think you're a poor fisherman, eventually you'll quit. And after you quit, if anyone ever asks you to go again, you'll say, "Not me, I hate fishing."

So what's the moral of the story? It's very important to think positive thoughts about who you are, because you'll seldom go beyond what you believe to be true about yourself. It's important to feel good about you as a person.

Let me ask you a question: When is the most important time to believe you're good at fishing? Answer: Before you actually are.

Question: When do you most need to believe you have what it takes to be good at tennis? Answer: The day you start to learn the game, when you're hitting balls everywhere but in your own court.

And when do you most need to feel that you've got a good mind and can bring up your grades? Answer: When your grades are not very good.

So here's the moral of the story: First we dream the dream and then we build the wings to make it fly.

CHAPTER THREE

Lighting the Fuse

I used to be a bishop, but I'm not sure how good at it I was because one time a youth said to me, "I used to think bishops were just about perfect, but you're not like that at all." Perhaps he meant that as a compliment. I suppose we'll never know.

While I was bishop, Larry, a young man in my ward, flunked his senior year of high school.

Because the bishop is also the president of the priests quorum, I thought that the priests and I ought to do something to try and help Larry. So our quorum purchased some copies of *The Memory Book* by Jerry Lucas and Harry Lorayne. This interesting book says that if you want to remember something all you have to do is create a cartoon about it in your head. The stranger the cartoon, the easier it is to memorize something.

We practiced memorizing every Wednesday night. Within a month, we could memorize an entire *Time* magazine. By that I mean we could tell you in general terms what was on every page in the magazine.

Just before school opened, our ward had a potluck supper. I don't know how potluck suppers are in your ward, but in ours, we set out long tables and all the people stand in line and wait to pick up their share of noodles.

Larry and I walked up to a man in line, handed him a copy of a current issue of *Time* magazine, and invited him to turn to any page. We said that without looking we'd be able to tell him what was on that page.

"All right, what's on page 38?" he asked.

Larry told him what was on page 38.

The man looked surprised. He probably figured Larry had just been lucky. "All right, what's on page 73?"

Larry told him what was on page 73.

The man, thinking Larry couldn't possibly know what was on every page, turned to the end of the magazine. "Page 98?"

Larry told him what was on page 98.

Suddenly he looked at Larry with the strangest expression, as if thinking, "Good grief, this kid's a genius."

Larry on the other hand was thinking, "He's looking at me like he thinks I'm a genius."

Within five minutes in a food line at a potluck supper, I saw a miracle happen. There was a noticeable change that came over Larry. It was like a light snapped on in his mind. Suddenly he knew he wasn't dumb—he could memorize better than anyone in that room.

We have two high schools in town. When school started, Larry switched high schools. He wanted to go where nobody knew him, where nobody, especially the teachers, thought he was dumb.

You can imagine what a teacher would think when a student walks into class, tosses a *Time* magazine on the desk, and says, "Turn to any page, and I'll tell you what's on that page."

In exams that year, Larry was awesome. You know the kind of question that says: "Yugoslavia has ten major industries. Name three." Larry would name all ten.

That school year he got all *A*'s and *B*'s. His teachers thought he was a genius. When he reached nineteen he went on a mission. He memorized hundreds of scriptures, including the Book of Matthew.

After his mission, he went to Ricks College, graduating with a 3.9 grade point average. He was chosen the most outstanding graduate from his discipline. Currently he attends BYU. The last time I talked to him he was considering going to graduate school to get a Ph.D.

Question: What happened to Larry at that ward supper? Did he grow more brain cells? Did he suddenly get smart? Was it the noodles? If not, what made the difference?

The answer's obvious. In discovering just one of his talents, Larry changed the way he thought about himself. The talent to memorize had gone unused for years. Because Larry didn't know it was there, he couldn't take advantage of it. It was buried treasure just waiting to be discovered. Once he found it, his life took on an exciting new direction.

What about you? Most people are aware of a few of their talents. But what if that's just scratching the surface? What if you haven't discovered your greatest talent yet?

I'd like to give you one more example. I call it the "Parable of the Brown Suit." Six years ago I was given a nearly new suit. The first time I wore it I noticed it had only one side pocket. The other was a fake pocket. For the next six years, I lived with this minor inconvenience.

A few months ago I was asked to be a substitute teacher for an early morning seminary class. On the day I was to teach the class, I put on my brown suit and then went to drop my hairbrush in the side pocket, only to discover that the pocket was full of cookie crumbs. And then I remembered being at a wedding reception a few days earlier. I had sampled one of the cookies, decided I didn't like it, and slipped it into my suit pocket. Since then the cookie had been crushed into a thousand crumbs.

You can't put a hairbrush into a pocket full of cookie crumbs, because if you do, after you brush your hair with it, people will think you have a very unusual form of brown dandruff.

Suddenly I got furious at whatever idiot company would design a suit with only one side pocket. I went to a drawer, got a pair of scissors, and attacked the fake pocket.

Guess what? It wasn't a fake pocket after all. The manufacturer had sewn it shut, and for the past six years, all I needed to do was cut one piece of thread and I would have had two pockets instead of just one. The pocket had been available for the past six years, but because I didn't believe it was there, it sat there unused.

What about you? What talents lie there unused in your life? Actually that's a question you can't answer. You don't know. That's why the talents are hidden. But I can guarantee you that God hasn't short-changed anyone. "For all have not every gift given unto them; for there are many gifts, and to every man is given a gift by the Spirit of God. To some is given one, and to some is given another, that all may be profited thereby." (D&C 46:11-12.)

Did you get that? To every person is given a gift. I believe that means not only spiritual gifts but also unique talents. God has done his part. Now all you have to do is find out what you've been given.

It's vitally important for you to believe that God has given you many talents. Unless you believe that, you might not ever make the effort to find out what your talents are. That would affect not only you but the many others who might benefit from the talents God has given you in order to bless the world.

So believe in yourself and be willing to discover what God has given you.

I think we can all learn a lesson from my brown suit—now with two side pockets.

The purpose of this book is to help you discover some

of your hidden talents. But you'll need to do a few things as you're reading this. It's not going to do much good to just read this and walk away, still full of vague desires to reach the stars but with no steps to get there.

So there's going to be some homework as we go along. I hope you'll do it. If you do, it will enrich your life.

I owe this exercise to Elder Hartman Rector, Jr., who taught it to us when he attended our stake conference a few years ago.

Homework

You're going to learn the Ten Commandments using memory gimmicks. This is what you'll do:

1. Think of one and only. *Thou shalt have no other gods before me.*

2. Think of zoo. In some zoos they have a statue of a lion. Two—think of zoo. *Thou shalt not make unto thee any graven image.*

3. Tree—A tree has leaves. A leaf has veins, which reminds us of vain. Three—think of tree. *Thou shalt not take the name of the Lord in vain.*

4. Think of door. A door has a keyhole; hole reminds us of holy. Four—think of door—keyhole—hole—holy. *Thou shalt keep the Sabbath Day holy.*

5. Think of drive. You are going on a drive with your parents. Five—think of drive. *Thou shalt honor your father and your mother.*

6. Think of sticks. You could kill someone by beating them with a stick. Six—think of sticks. *Thou shalt not kill.*

7. Think of heaven. If you want to go to heaven, don't commit adultery. Seven—think of heaven. *Thou shalt not commit adultery.*

8. Think of gate. The reason to put up gates is to keep robbers away. Eight—think of gate. *Thou shalt not steal.*

9. Nine—think of lying. *Thou shalt not bear false witness.*

10. Think of hen. Your neighbor has a chicken and you'd like to take it and eat it. You covet your neighbor's chicken. Ten—think of hen. *Thou shalt not covet.*

Have you got all ten? Have someone quiz you and see how well you do.

Of course you can use this technique to remember anything. All you need is a distinct cartoon in your mind that will help you link it to what you want to remember. For example, you can learn words from a foreign language, such as French, this same way. The following is from *The Memory Book*:

Bread—*pan* (pan). The handle of a pan is a loaf of French bread.

Beans—*haricots* (ah-ree-koh). Millions of beans are wearing hairy coats.

Snails—*escargots* (ess-cahr-go). A gigantic snail is carrying a cargo of S's.

Duck—*canard* (ka-nar). Someone throws a can hard, and you duck.

Cake—*gateau* (gah-toh). A gigantic birthday cake has got you by the toe.

Chicken—*poulet* (poo-lay). You're pulling the leg of a gigantic chicken.

CHAPTER FOUR

Get Out There and Fail

This is from a scene in one of my stories published in the *New Era* that later became the BYU-produced movie *The Phone Call*. Here Scott talks to Becky at the drive-in restaurant where they both work. Scott starts it off.

"If I lettered in football, then I'd be somebody. I'd have a red R on my jacket. When I walked down the street, people would stop and say, 'Look, he's got a letter on his jacket.' Then I'd be somebody, and Pam would go out with me."

"You're somebody now. You just haven't realized it."

"If I was just better at speaking to people. My dad talks to people all the time. Even gas station attendants. He just walks up and starts talking. By the time the tank's full, they're old friends."

"You can learn," she said. "Talk to the customers."

"Why not?" he answered.

A few minutes later a Volkswagen with two college girls from California stopped for burgers and fries and drinks. Becky cooked the burgers and fries while Scott got the drinks ready.

"Nice day, isn't it?" Scott leaned over the counter to talk to one of the girls.

"Yeah."

"Tell me, how are things in California? Are the oranges doing well?"

"What?" the startled girl asked, upset by the intense manner with which Scott spoke to her.

"The oranges in California. How're they doing?"

"I dunno."

Scott leaned further out, straining to catch some threads of sanity in the conversation. "I guess if they weren't doing well, we'd have heard."

Now almost shouting, Scott continued. "I mean, since we haven't heard, we can assume we'll have a good crop of oranges this year." Almost as a command, he barked out, "Wouldn't you say that?"

The girl backed away.

"I see you're driving a Volkswagen. How's the gas mileage?"

"I'm not sure."

"I think that's funny!" Scott yelled, looking every bit like an escaped lunatic. "You got a small car so you'd get good gas mileage. And yet you don't even know what gas mileage you're getting. Don't you think that's funny? Well, don't you?" Scott barked, his voice cracking.

"Please can we have our food?" one of the girls pleaded.

As soon as the food and money exchanged hands, the girls ran to the car and drove off, missing the driveway and going over the curb.

Scott and Becky watched them speed off. "Now you see what I mean. I never say the right thing. That's why I'm so afraid to call Pam. I'd mess the whole thing up."

As you can see, Scott's first attempt at talking to the customers didn't work out very well. But after the hundredth time, he'll probably get the hang of it. He just needs a little more practice.

We're in this life to get experience. The Lord told Joseph Smith: "Know thou, my son, that all these things shall give thee experience, and shall be for thy good." (D&C 122:7.)

Why are most of us afraid of gaining experience by trying something new? It's usually because we don't want to look foolish. We're afraid people will make fun of us. We feel more comfortable only doing the things we do well. That's too bad in a way, because, like it or not, failure is a great teacher.

Let's take an example. When you were four years old, you probably missed the first time you tried to catch a ball. You may have also missed the second time and the third time and the fourth time—maybe even the twenty-ninth time. Let's say that on the sixtieth try you finally caught the ball.

Shall we add this up? Failures: 59. Successes: 1.

Does that mean you're a failure at age four? Of course not, because each of those fifty-nine failures has taught you something about catching a ball. For the next one hundred tosses maybe you'll catch four of them. After another hundred tosses, you'll catch ten. After the next hundred tosses, you'll catch thirty.

Now let's add this up. Failures: 315. Successes: 45. You're doing great even though failures still outnumber successes.

A major league baseball player is considered a star if he gets 350 hits out of 1,000 times at bat. And for this he may be paid two hundred thousand dollars a year. And yet out of those 1,000 times at bat, he fails 650 times, nearly twice as often as he succeeds.

So don't be afraid of making mistakes, because they're often stepping stones to success.

Most self-help books tell you to get out there and

succeed. This book, at least in this chapter, is telling you to get out there and fail.

Homework

In order to discover our talents, we need to try a lot of things just to see which ones we enjoy the most. Of course whenever we do something for the first time, we'll make some mistakes. Some people will view that as failure, but it really is growth.

In this homework assignment, concentrate on the kind of a person you aren't. That is, read through the list of activities and choose some you would ordinarily be the least likely to do. Do those first. Why? Because in order to discover your hidden talents, you need to get out of the rut you're in and try new things. Even if it's in an area you later decide you have little talent for, just doing something new will build your self-confidence.

1. *Learn to play two songs on the piano.*

You don't need to take piano lessons to learn two songs on the piano. Go to a music store and find out where they keep the easy sheet music. Pick out two songs. Then ask a very patient friend or relative who plays the piano to show you where to put your fingers for each measure of the song. It may take a few weeks, but eventually you can learn how to play the entire song.

After you've mastered your first song, learn the other. Two songs are all you'll need your entire life.

If you're a single guy, let me explain how this will improve your life. Let's say you have a date. You go to the girl's house, and she isn't ready. You notice her family has a piano, so you ask her parents if it'd be all right if you play the piano while you wait. They say sure, so you sit down and play your first song.

Her dad is thinking, "Wow, this guy isn't like all the others. He's got class."

Your date comes into the living room while you're playing. She's impressed. She asks you to play another song, and so you play your second song. Have you got the picture? There you are sitting at the piano, and your date and her parents are looking at you with admiration.

"That's so good," your date says when you finish. "Play another song."

But you've only learned two songs, so what do you do? You look at your watch and say, "Well, we really ought to be going now."

Two songs—that's all you'll need your entire life.

How do I know? Because my wife taught me to play two songs, even though I don't really know how to play the piano. My first song is "Feelings." I've played it before hundreds of people. Once during the weekend of general conference, I played it on the grand piano in the crowded lobby of the Hotel Utah—until the desk clerk came over and told me to stop because I was bothering the guests.

But that's not the point. The point is that once you do even as simple a thing as this, you'll be more confident that you can do other things you've never done before.

If you're a girl and you learn two songs, it works the same way, except that when your date rings the doorbell, you're already at the piano. Let your parent or roommate answer the door.

"Don't stop," your date says as he comes in while you're playing. You finish playing your first song for him. He's impressed. "Hey, that's great! Play another one."

You play your second song and then say, "Well, we'd better get going."

If you don't have a piano in your home, then practice on a friend's piano or see if you can get permission to practice on the one at church. Then when you're on a date, wait until you get near a piano to play your two songs.

The only problem will be if your date has also read this. Then you both will play your two songs for each other and end up being late for the movie.

2. Create your own artwork and place it in a prominent place in your living room.

We're not talking art lessons here. We're talking slapping out a modern art painting in a couple of afternoons.

Go to an art supply store and buy some paint and a canvas to paint on. Or if money's tight, haunt the church bulletin board until one of the posters becomes outdated, and then ask the bishop, "Does anybody care if I take down this old poster?"

Now it's time to be creative. Slap the paint down any way you want. For example, go out in the garage and borrow your brother's tricycle. Put paint on its wheels, set the canvas down, and roll the tricycle all over the canvas. Or drop the paint onto the canvas from a ladder. Experiment with colors until you have a spectacularly colorful hodgepodge. Then buy or make yourself a nice frame.

If you're living at home, let your parents know you'd be really insulted if they didn't let you hang your painting in the living room. After it's hung, aim all the lamps in the room toward the painting so it becomes the most noticeable thing in the room.

Okay, your picture is hung. Friends come over, and they see the painting. (How could they miss it?) What do they say? "Gee, that's an . . . interesting painting."

"Oh that?" you say nonchalantly. "I did that myself."

Their eyes open wide in amazement. "*You* painted that?"

"Oh, sure."

"I didn't know you were an artist."

"Well, I did do that painting."

Now how will that make you feel? Great! Just doing this one simple thing will build your self-confidence. Why? Because normally you don't paint, but now you have. Since you've done that, maybe there's some other things you've never done that you can do too.

Sometimes we get so hung up on excellence that we overlook the value of doing something just for the fun of it. It's better to turn out a mediocre first painting than never to have painted anything.

Don't feel like you have to be perfect at everything. No writer or artist sits down with the idea that the next project will be a classic, perfect in every way. You can't create and be a critic at the same time.

So paint your painting. It can't do any harm, can it? And what if in doing it, you discover something about yourself. What if you absolutely love art? What if art is the thing you spent those ten thousand years doing? If that's true, then look out, you're on your way.

The truth is that you don't discover your talents, they discover you. And when that happens, nobody will be able to stop you from developing your talent. Time will seem to stand still. You'll look at your watch, and it will be 3:00. Five minutes later you'll look again, and it will be 6:15. You won't know where the time has gone.

A year ago I gave a talk about talents at a single adult conference. A few months later I received a letter from a woman who had attended the conference. Here is an excerpt from her letter: "You encouraged me to try many things until I found something that I could really get excited about. . . . Well in December I bought a Casiotone for the children and me to play with. Only I found out that I couldn't leave it alone, so I started taking lessons the twenty-ninth of December. Well to make a long story short, I have been taking lessons for two months and in that time I have gone through the equivalent of eighteen months of lessons. I found out what you meant by the strange excitement that makes you really lose track of time. I try and practice for an hour or more a day, and now I can hear things in music I couldn't before. I find myself wanting to study the great masters like Beethoven, Mozart, Schubert, and others."

Cracker Jacks used to have an interesting slogan. "The more you eat, the more you want." Life is like that too. Whenever you learn to do something, you gain confidence, which helps you do something else you've never done, which gives you more self-confidence. And on and on and on it goes. The more you do, the more you can do. Nothing you ever do or learn will go to waste. It's all useful. The only thing that isn't useful is not doing anything.

3. *Learn to cook one elegant meal.*

You should learn how to prepare at least one elegant meal. It should be something you can serve by candlelight, with soft music playing in the background.

One good meal, that's all it takes. As you cycle through your various dates, you can prepare your one good meal for each of them.

We're not talking cheeseburger and fries here. How about a tossed salad, a cooked vegetable, a nice cut of meat, some homemade rolls, a baked potato, and maybe a flashy dessert. It doesn't matter what it is as long as it's done with style.

If you're a guy, let me explain why learning to cook one fancy supper will help you.

First of all, we need to face facts. Times are changing, and cooking can no longer be considered only woman's work. If you insist on thinking that it is, you're going to offend a lot of people.

Most likely, right after you get married, your wife will have a job too. Any bright young woman today will naturally be curious to know if a prospective husband is going to expect her to work eight hours a day and then come home and fix dinner, just because he has some prehistoric idea that cooking is woman's work. And so if you invite her over and prepare an elegant meal, you'll almost be able to hear her sigh of relief as she realizes that you aren't hung up on outdated role models.

When you take time to prepare a meal for your date, it's a way of saying you value her enough to take the time necessary to prepare the lettuce, chop the tomatoes, dice the potatoes, and simmer the vegetables.

If you're a single young woman, you should learn to prepare one elegant meal too. Not just to impress a guy with your domestic skills, but also because it's a way of doing some testing of your own.

Beware of the guy whose entire food vocabulary is "cheeseburger and fries." If you were to marry a guy like that, he might never appreciate the finer things in life; savoring the smell of the air after a rainstorm, walking along the beach in the morning, or reaching out and holding your hand—even after forty years of marriage.

You're not Burger King. In future years you won't want your husband to come up and say, "Two kisses and an embrace to go. Oh yeah, hold the tenderness. I'm kind of in a hurry." That's why you need to see how a guy handles a leisurely classy meal, because some of the nicest things in life take time.

4. *Learn how to draw using your right brain.*

There's a book you might enjoy called *Drawing on the Right Side of the Brain,* by Dr. Betty Edwards. It says that our brain is roughly divided in two parts. The left brain handles verbal, logical, and analytical thinking. It deals with symbols. The right brain is more mellow; it deals with images and dreams and intuition.

By the time we reach junior high school, our left brain

has taken over because most formal education is usually left-brain oriented. So when we're asked to draw a chair, our left brain says, "Hey, let's get on with it! Don't take all day. Here, this is the symbol for a chair." And the left brain has the hand draw this terrible sketch of a chair without even looking at what a chair looks like. For example, the left brain knows that every leg of a chair is the same length. So when it's in charge of drawing a chair, it makes each leg the same length, even though when we look at a chair from an angle its legs don't look the same length.

On the other hand, the right brain is very patient and would be quite willing to study the details of each and every chair and faithfully draw what is seen. And it would do it if only the left brain weren't so bossy.

The strategy suggested by Dr. Edwards is to give the left brain a job that it either can't or doesn't want to do. For example, if you want to draw a photograph, turn the photograph upside down. The left brain says, "That's stupid. I'm not drawing something upside down." It figuratively storms away, insulted that we'd ask it to do such a dumb thing.

The right brain says, "Hey, I'll do it." Without the bossy left brain around, the right brain takes its time to consider each detail of the photograph and then tries to reproduce it on paper.

But of course if your brother asks you to draw a picture of him, you probably won't be able to get him to stand on his head for half an hour while you draw. So what do you do? Simple. Instead of drawing your brother's face, focus your attention on the edge of space between your brother and the air.

Your left brain will protest that it's not going to draw the air boundary around somebody's face. That leaves your right brain free to go ahead.

For this homework assignment, you should take a picture from a magazine, turn it upside down, and draw it. Then draw the same picture right side up. Compare the two and decide which is better. You could also check out *Drawing on the Right Side of the Brain* from the library. Read it and do the exercises.

5. Go out for a team sport.

In most schools, less than ten percent of the students go out for a sport. Why don't the rest? Because they know they'll get cut from the team.

What if you went out for a varsity sport knowing full well you weren't going to make the team? You might ask yourself, "Why would a person do that?" Look at it this way. For one full week you'll get to wear the school's sweats. They'll keep everything washed for you too. You'll get free showers for a week, and the use of the whirlpool. With any luck you'll get out of some chores at home.

You'll gain some new friends. Everyone else will be under a lot of pressure to make the team. But not you, because you already know you're not going to make it. Therefore, you can be good sport and encourage everybody and cheer them on.

Just going out for a sport puts you way above the ones who didn't dare to try. The person who tries is always better off than the person who doesn't. Failure isn't the worst thing in the world. Not trying is worser. (Sorry about the grammar.)

Caution: Before you actually go out for a team sport, get parental consent and your family physician's approval.

6. Learn how to work a difficult math problem.

Some people are afraid of mathematics. Yet before we came to earth, I'll bet we weren't afraid of anything. I think we must have picked up our fears since we came here.

If a teacher asks you to read one hundred pages of history, you have to spend a certain amount of time on it no matter what. But with math, if you can figure out an easy way, you can be done with your homework in five minutes. That's why I liked math in school.

Here's a problem. Once you know the trick, it's simple.

You've got two trains. We'll call one of them Train A and the other Train B. They begin 200 miles apart on the same track, and move toward each other at a speed of 50 miles an hour.

There's also a bird that flies 60 miles an hour. It flies from Train A to Train B and then reverses direction and flies back to Train A. It flies from one train to the other, over and over again, until the two trains collide.

Question: How far will the bird fly before the trains collide?

The reason why this is a hard question is because the trains keep moving closer and closer, and so the distance the bird has to travel between trains keeps getting shorter and shorter.

But sometimes if we will look at something in a different way, we'll find out that even the hardest problems aren't so bad after all.

What if we forget about the bird for a minute and focus our attention on the trains. How much time will it take before the trains collide?

Well, let's see, the trains are 200 miles apart and are traveling the same speed. They'll meet in the middle. So that means each train will travel 100 miles, which is the middle of 200. If the trains are traveling 50 miles an hour, it'll take 2 hours to travel the 100 miles.

Now let's go back to the bird. If it flies 60 miles an hour and flies for 2 hours, it will fly 120 miles.

This is a tough problem, so you may have to read through it a couple of times to really understand it. But don't worry if you don't understand it right away. Maybe mathematics isn't one of the things you worked on for ten thousand years before you were born.

7. *Learn scriptures from the Doctrine and Covenants using memory tricks.*

Here's some memory tricks. See how you like them.

A. The Word of Wisdom is found in section 89. To remember this, think of this statement: "Some fool ate the wine." "Ate the wine" will remind you of eighty-nine.

B. The section of the Doctrine and Covenants that explains about temple marriage is section 132. Just remember that getting married in the temple is as easy as 1-3-2. If it were really easy, it would be as easy as 1-2-3. It's a little harder than 1-2-3, so it's 1-3-2.

C. A reference to tithing is found in D&C 119. Just think of the words *one fun dime.* Since tithing is ten percent, or a dime out of every dollar, with any luck that'll remind you of one-one-nine.

D. Encouraging parents to teach their children is found in section 68. To remember this, think of the words *sticky gate.* How did the gate get sticky? By children who'd eaten candy just before going through the gate. Sticky gate reminds you of sixty-eight.

It's easier to remember things with memory tricks. Think of a memory trick to help you remember something you need to know for an exam.

8. *Become a good dancer.*

Once I was asked to chaperon a youth temple excursion to the Cardston Temple in Canada. While there, we attended a stake dance. Since we were from the States, everyone thought we knew all the latest fads. As a joke, we

made up a dance and told them that everyone in California was doing it. It was kind of a dumb dance actually,
but before we left we had everyone doing it.

After that I never worried about dancing, because I
realized the secret to dancing is to look like you know
what you're doing.

Here are some possible titles for dances: The Big Mac,
The Statue of Liberty, The BYU Quarterback Passing
Dance. See if you can make up some actions to the titles.
The next time you have a dance, teach them to some
unsuspecting friends.

9. Do a simple science demonstration.

If you let a can of tomato juice and a can of tomato
paste roll down a hill together, which one will reach the
bottom first? First guess and then try it. (If you don't have
tomato juice, use a container of salt and a bottle of water.)

Which one wins? The tomato juice. Does it depend on
which one is heavier? No. Does it depend on which one is
bigger? No.

Here's the explanation. At the top of the hill, each
object has what we call potential energy. Potential energy
just means that they have energy because they're at the
top of the hill. As they roll down the hill, they change their
potential energy to kinetic energy. Kinetic energy is energy
of motion.

For any rolling object, there are two kinds of kinetic
energy. One kind is called translational, the energy that
an object has as it moves through space. The other kind of
kinetic energy is called rotational. For a rolling object,
these two energies are both important. The more rotational kinetic energy an object has, the less translational
kinetic energy it can have. This also works the other way
around.

Now let's talk about the can of tomato juice. The trick

to understanding what's going on is that a liquid won't rotate as the can rolls down the hill. That means the rotational kinetic energy is small, which makes its translational kinetic energy (the energy that moves an object through space) big.

But the tomato paste is almost a solid, and so it'll rotate as the can rolls, which makes the rotational kinetic energy a greater fraction of the total energy. Therefore, it won't move down the hill as fast as the tomato juice.

Tomato juice beats tomato paste every time.

But what would happen if you froze the tomato juice? Or what if you roll a ball and a hoop down a hill, which one will win? Try it and see. This is kind of fun, right?

Sometimes in beginning courses it's easy to get the idea that science is just a lot of facts to be memorized. But science research can be a lot of fun. Maybe you'd like it.

If you're a girl, you should know that there's a great need right now for young women to go into science to provide role models for future generations. If all the scientists in the world are men, then we've lost out on half of the discoveries we might have made.

I wrote a novel, *A New Dawn*, about a twenty-two-year-old young woman who discovers a theory Einstein spent the last thirty years of his life searching for.

This scene occurs in the laundry room of a large apartment building near Princeton University:

Lisa drowsily stared at the clothes spinning in the dryer, still slipping in and out of consciousness.

Then it happened.

Out of nowhere, on the edge of sleep, she saw a mathematical term jump into place in one of the equations she'd been agonizing over. Suddenly she realized she had the answer that'd eluded Einstein. She knew how to unify all the forces in the universe into one set of equations. She'd found a mathematical quantity that, like a key, opened the universe.

"I've got it," she mumbled, still in a daze. "I never thought I'd get it, but I finally did. Now I've got it."

A girl eyed her suspiciously. "No kidding. It's not contagious, is it?" She moved two chairs away.

Lisa looked around for paper and pencil, but she'd left everything upstairs.

"Do you have any paper?" she asked the girl.

"No, why?"

"I've got to capture it before it leaves."

A girl looked at Lisa's dryer. "It's bolted down—it's not gonna leave."

Lisa opened the dryer and took out two white sheets. "Do you have a pen or pencil?"

"No."

"Do you have lipstick in your purse?"

"What shade?"

"It doesn't matter."

"Well ... I usually don't lend it out. You wouldn't believe what some people do to the point."

"Lend me your lipstick!"

"All right, all right. You don't have to shout."

The girl handed it over. Lisa fell to the floor and tried to write on the sheet with it.

"I swear, the weirdos they got in this place ..."

The lipstick broke in two.

"Somehow I knew you'd do that."

"What else have you got?"

The girl looked through her purse and came up with a Magic Marker. Lisa grabbed it, knelt on the floor, and began writing on the sheet.

"Hey, you just can't go around using people's Magic Markers."

"I have to get it down while it's fresh."

"While what's fresh? The sheet? You don't write on dirty sheets, is that it?"

Lisa kept writing. . . . She filled one sheet and then started on the other. In a few minutes, it was full too. She grabbed a blouse from the dryer and began writing on it. When she finished with that, she looked over at the girl's clothes swishing in the washing machine.

"Oh no, you don't!" The girl pulled her soaking wet clothes out of the washer and ran out of the room.

Lisa grabbed the sheets and blouse and hurried to her apartment. Once inside, she rushed to her desk and began transcribing the equations from the sheets onto paper. The equations proceeded in logical order, each one leading to the other. Tears streamed down her face. The equations revealed order and harmony in the universe.

10. *Learn the basics of car maintenance.*

You'll be dependent on a car your entire life, so you might as well learn a few things about how to keep it running.

Get someone who knows about cars to teach you how to change a tire, change the oil, clean the battery terminals, jump start a car, or change spark plugs.

11. *Learn how to juggle.*

Everyone loves a juggler. Get someone to teach you.

CHAPTER FIVE

Getting Rid of Your Bad News Coach

"Report to my office when you're dressed," the coach growled to Dan in the locker room after the practice.

A short time later, Dan sheepishly stood in front of the coach's desk.

"I'm dropping you from the team," the coach said.

"Why? I take good care of my uniform. I keep all the training rules. Why drop me?"

"Because you can't play football!" the coach roared. (From "The Emergence of Butterflies," a short story by Jack Weyland.)

It'd be tough to play for a coach who was always grumpy, never said anything nice, and only remembered the bad plays you made.

The truth is I carry someone like that around with me. He lives in my mind, and he's a real grouch. I call him my Bad News Coach.

When I first started thinking about writing, my Bad News Coach was against the whole idea. (He's usually against everything.) "What makes you think you can write?" he said. "A writer ought to have a degree in English. Well all right, if you must, go ahead, write me a sentence. Oh c'mon, give me a break. You call that a sentence? That's garbage. Write something else. I can't believe it! That's even worse. Look, you can't write. Give up before you make an even worse fool out of yourself."

To find out if you have a Bad News Coach too, answer the following questions:

1. *What do you do when someone compliments you?*

If you turn it aside or try to talk the person out of it, then that may be your Bad News Coach talking.

For example, if a friend says, "Gee, your hair looks nice today," do you answer, "Are you kidding? I haven't washed it in a week."

It's as if you want to talk your friend out of the compliment. Why do that? If you pour cold water on the nice things people say about you, you're doing yourself an injustice, and everytime you do that, you've given your Bad News Coach a little more power.

What's the best answer when someone gives you a compliment? That's simple—just say "thanks."

2. *Do you ever call yourself names?*

The Bad News Coach loves to stick labels on us, labels that may stay with us for our entire lives. If we ever spill something or fall down, our Bad News Coach labels us with "You're clumsy." And if we don't fight it, we'll go around carrying the label "clumsy" around our neck. If we believe that label, what will happen if someone asks us to go play softball? We'll say no. Why? Because we believe we're clumsy, just because years ago we tripped in front of some people who laughed at us. And so the Bad News Coach puts us in a mental jail, boxed in by the labels he's hung around our necks long ago.

If five years ago someone said you were clumsy, that doesn't mean you are now or even that you were then. If one time you flunked a course, that doesn't mean you're dumb. If someone calls you ugly, that doesn't mean you are.

Don't let others label you, and avoid hanging negative labels on yourself. They're simply not true.

3. *What do you say to yourself when something goes wrong?*

See if any of these comments sound familiar:

a. "That's just my luck."

b. "I knew this wouldn't work out."

c. "I never should have tried this."

d. "Nothing ever goes my way."

e. "I never do anything right."

Have you got a Bad News Coach too? Where did this grouch come from anyway? Not the preexistence, that's for sure. We must have picked him/her up since we were born. It's too bad, because if we've got a Bad News Coach feeding us a steady stream of negative messages, it makes life pretty tough sometimes.

We've taken this abuse long enough. Isn't it time to send our Bad News Coach packing?

First we need to separate the past from the present. Here's what Richard L. Evans observed: "The past has its place and is valuable for lessons learned. The present also has its place, and what we cannot change should not needlessly keep us from looking and moving forward. Nothing lost or left behind should keep us from becoming what we can become, from learning what we now can learn.

"There are new decisions every day, every hour, and reasons to improve and to repent. Whatever we are, wherever we've been, each day we have some opportunity to determine our direction. . . .

"Whatever the past or its meaning, or its length, or its

losses, or its lessons learned or left unlearned—whatever it is—we go on from where we are—wherever it is—and become what we can become; with work, repentance, improvement; with faith in the future."

The simple fact is that God doesn't want you to feel bad about yourself. He wants you to have joy. (See 2 Nephi 2:25.) Father in Heaven is the most positive, upbeat, encouraging, loving, concerned father we can imagine.

Listen to this. "Verily I say, men should be anxiously engaged in a good cause, and *do many things of their own free will, and bring to pass much righteousness; for the power is in them, wherein they are agents unto themselves.* And inasmuch as men do good they shall in nowise lose their reward." (D&C 58:27-28; italics added.)

Did you get that? You can do many wonderful things. What's even better, the power is in *you* to do it. God gave you that power. You are one of his children, and so by the laws of heredity, the power is in you to become the kind of creative, loving, open, warm, and effective person God wants you to be.

So if the Bad News Coach is telling you you're no good, get yourself a new coach.

Want to hear how the Good News Coach sounds? Let's say a teacher hands back your exam and it has a big *D* written on the top in red.

We already know what the Bad News Coach would say, "Hey, Airhead, can't you do anything right?"

Getting back the same exam with a *D* on it, the Good News Coach talks quietly and respectfully to us. "That's too bad. I bet you're disappointed. It looks like you haven't quite mastered the material yet. It's not the end of the world though. There's another test in a week. I'm sure that if you spend a little more time studying, you'll do much better next time."

The Good News Coach is much gentler and doesn't call us names.

Homework

1. *Quit trying to talk people out of it when they compliment you. Accept compliments with a simple thank-you.*

> Let's try it:
> Someone says, "You look great today."
> You say, "Thanks."
> Someone else says, "You're so much fun to be around."
> What's your answer?
> "Thank you."
> Now one more time.
> "You did a great job on your talk in church today."
> And what do you say?
> "Thanks!"

2. *Make a list of your good qualities.*

Most people can think of only a few of their good qualities, but at the same time they can fill pages with a list of their shortcomings. That's not fair. It's time to balance things up.

What are some good things about your face? If you can't think of any, ask your mother. Mothers usually know nice things about their children's faces.

What are some things you appreciate about your body? Do you have long fingers so you can play the piano? Can you run fast? Are you good at sports? Do you learn physical skills easily? Do you like to dance? What are some things you like about your hair?

What about your mind? Can you figure out "Wheel of Fortune" phrases before the contestants can? Can you draw well? Can you figure out how a piece of machinery works? Do you know how to visualize things in three dimensions? Can you think of funny things to say? Have you learned how to program a computer? Was it easy for you to learn how to drive? Are you good at puzzles? Do you know how to play chess? Do you enjoy reading?

Come up with your own list.

What about your spirituality? Have you felt the influence of the Holy Ghost? Do you ever get the feeling that you know something that someone says in church is true? When you pray do you feel that God is listening? Have you ever had a patriarchal blessing? What are some nice things God has to say about you in that blessing? Are you able to fast on fast Sunday? Do you ever bear your testimony? Have you ever read the Book of Mormon? List some spiritual qualities that you have.

How are you around people? Do people ever tell you their problems because you help them feel better? Can you make people laugh? Can you sense how others are feeling?

What about learning? Is it easy for you to grasp a new skill? Can you visualize how something you're building will look when it's finished? Can you see where something is on a page even days after you've read it? What are your favorite subjects in school? What skill activities do you enjoy the most?

What do you like doing on a Saturday afternoon with nothing else to do?

How important is music in your life? Do you play a musical instrument? Can you sing along to the words of songs on the radio?

Are you able to fix things when they break down? Are you the kind of person parents are able to trust with the most important thing in their lives—their children? They show that trust everytime they ask you to baby-sit.

3. *Ask a parent or a friend to make a list of some of your good qualities. Read the list once a day for a week.*

I can almost hear you saying, "I can't do that."

Why not? If you don't think you're worthwhile, it doesn't matter what anyone else thinks. If you've gone around for years with a steady stream of negative thoughts about yourself, it's time to reverse the trend.

4. *For the next week whenever you're in a group that's gossiping about someone, instead of joining in, say something nice about that person.*

You can't be positive about yourself and at the same time be critical of those around you. If you talk about others, you will store those same words and someday you'll use them on yourself.

So if you want to feel better about yourself, you have to treat others better too. The Savior understood this when he said, "Love your neighbor as yourself." We can't love ourselves unless we love those around us. The more comfortable we feel about ourselves, the easier it will be to show love to others.

Let's try a practical example. You're sitting in the school cafeteria. A friend next to you says, "Hey, look at dumbo over there. He just spilled his milk all over the table. Hey! Way to go, Klutz!"

Can you see yourself saying, "Everybody spills milk some time. It's no big deal."

5. *Stop rehashing your past mistakes.*

Whenever you start thinking about a mistake you've made, stop yourself in the middle of it and start thinking positively about yourself.

If you insist upon reliving the past, add circus music to the rerun in your mind. Make the picture smaller or run it in fast forward, or even backwards.

Don't let yourself be held hostage to the past.

There are some mistakes that are more serious than missing a free throw in a basketball game. We'll talk more about serious mistakes, and the way to resolve them, in chapter 9.

6. *After talking it over with your parents and bishop, consider getting your patriarchal blessing.*

Heavenly Father has known you a long time, but because you can't remember your premortal existence, you've only known yourself over the span of a few years. So whose judgment about the kind of person you really are is more reliable—yours or God's?

If Heavenly Father could talk to you now, what advice would he give you about your life? A patriarchal blessing is revelation from God to you about your life.

Patriarchal blessings are sacred. Those who receive them should be faithful and mature.

Mine has been a great influence in my life. I have read it hundreds of times since I first received it.

A patriarchal blessing is a gift from God to you to let you know he loves and appreciates you. Talk to your bishop and your parents about receiving a patriarchal blessing.

As I close this chapter, I'd like to pass on some wise counsel from President Gordon B. Hinckley. At the 1983 BYU-Hawaii commencement exercises, he made the following statement:

"I am asking that we stop seeking out the storms and enjoy more fully the sunlight. I am suggesting that as we go through life we 'accentuate the positive.' I am asking that we look a little deeper for the good, that we still voices of insult and sarcasm, that we more generously compliment virtue and effort. I am not asking that all criticism be silenced. Growth comes of correction. Strength comes of repentance. Wise is the man who can acknowledge mistakes pointed out by others and change his course.

"What I am suggesting is that each of us turn from the negativism that so permeates our society and look for the remarkable good among those with whom we associate, that we speak of one another's virtues more than we speak of one another's faults, that optimism replace pessimism, that our faith exceed our fears. When I was a young man and was prone to speak critically, my father would say: 'Cynics do not contribute, skeptics do not create, doubters do not achieve.'"

CHAPTER SIX

You Gotta Have a Dream

There's a song in the musical *South Pacific* that gives some great advice. It says that we can't make our dreams come true if we don't even have any. I agree, "you gotta have a dream."

In 1936 Jesse Owens won four gold medals in the Olympic Games held in Germany. He was born in 1913 on a tenant farm in northern Alabama. He was one of seven children and worked in the cotton fields with his parents.

What made the difference in Jesse Owens's life? It happened when he was thirteen years old. His junior high school coach arranged to have Charles Paddock, the United States sprinter who'd just come back from the 1920 Olympics, speak at a school assembly. At that time he was known as the World's Fastest Human Being.

After the assembly, the coach asked Jesse what he thought about Mr. Paddock. Jesse thought about it for a moment and then said, "Well, gee, coach, I sure would like to be known as the World's Fastest Human Being."

The coach turned to Jesse and said: "Everybody should have a dream. Every man must remember that dreams are high and that you must climb a ladder to reach them. Each rung of that ladder has a meaning of its own as you climb. The first rung of that ladder, of course, goes back to one important point—just how dedicated are you? How much of what you have are you willing to give to the dream? And the next rung of the ladder is your determination to train yourself to reach the dream at the top. And the third rung of that ladder is the self-discipline that you must display in order to accomplish this. The fourth rung, which is one of the most important rungs in that ladder to your dreams, is the kind of attitude you have in going about all this. By this I mean are you capable of giving every moment that you possibly can to making this dream come true and of throwing your whole heart and soul into the effort?"

That day was the beginning of the journey that led Jesse Owens, thirteen years later, to win four Olympic gold medals. That was the day Jesse Owens acquired his dream, the day he decided that someday he would compete in the Olympics and also be known as the World's Fastest Human Being.

First we get ourselves a dream, and then we work out a plan to make it come true. We'll be working on both of these in this chapter.

John Goddard is a member of The Church of Jesus Christ of Latter-day Saints, and has shown the entire world how to get the most out of life. He was even the subject of a *Life* magazine article in 1972.

While still a young man of fifteen, he listed 127 goals on a sheet of paper. At the time of the article in 1972, he had achieved 103 of those goals. I have every reason to believe that he has achieved even more of them by now.

In the article he said, "When I was fifteen, all the adults I knew seemed to complain, 'Oh, if only I'd done this or that when I was younger.' They had let life slip by them. I was sure that if I planned for it, I could have a life of excitement and fun and knowledge."

And that he did. In 1951 he became the first man to explore the entire length of the Nile River by kayak. He is now a celebrated adventurer-lecturer.

His earliest accomplishments were the easiest ones: learning to type; becoming an Eagle Scout; learning to play the piano, the flute, and violin; riding a horse in the Rose Parade; going on a mission; building his own telescope; running a mile in five minutes; and learning to water and snow ski.

As he moved down his list, his goals got very difficult, but he still accomplished them: exploring the Nile River; studying primitive cultures in the Congo; climbing Mount Kilimanjaro and Mount Ararat; learning to fly a plane; photographing Victoria Falls in Rhodesia; visiting the Taj Mahal; skin diving to forty feet, and holding his breath underwater for two and a half minutes; publishing an article in *National Geographic*; learning to speak French, Spanish, and Arabic; reading the works of Shakespeare, Plato, Aristotle, Dickens, Thoreau, Rousseau, Hemingway, Twain, Burroughs, Talmage, Tolstoy, Longfellow, Keats, Poe, Bacon, Whittier, and Emerson; becoming proficient in the use of a plane, motorcycle, tractor, surfboard, rifle, pistol, canoe, microscope, football, basketball, bow and arrow, lariat, and boomerang; and retracing the travels of Marco Polo and Alexander the Great. These are only a partial list of all Mr. Goddard wanted to accomplish—and did.

At the time of the article, he was still working on visiting every country in the world, reading the entire *Encyclopedia Brittanica*; and visiting the moon.

One reason people don't get out of life what they want to is because they don't know what they want.

What do you want out of life? What kind of person do you want to be? *Now's* the time to decide.

Homework

Get a notebook and write down everything you want to do in your life. If you want to go to Hawaii someday, write it down. If you want to become a doctor, engineer, musician, mechanic, truck driver, artist, judge, lumberjack, writer, accountant, or senator, write it down. If you want to learn how to ski, write it down. Whatever it is you want to do, write it down.

The list should include not only what you want to do, but what you want to be: honest, virtuous, or courageous. Write it down. Do you want to serve a mission? How about a marriage in the temple? Write them down.

Don't write all these things down because someone else is going to be impressed when they read your list. In fact, don't plan on showing the list to anyone else. It's just for you.

Fill the entire notebook if you want. Write it down. Write it all down.

I'm in no hurry, I'll wait for you to get done.

You made the list, right? I hope so. It's important that you do.

Now what we do is use our list to make some movies in our minds. Let's take one of the items on your list. Since I don't know what's on your list, I'll take one I hope is there—getting married in the temple.

Make a movie in your mind of your temple wedding. Which temple is it going to be? Pick one, because we need some detail in your movie. You get out of the car and walk up the stairs to the doors of the temple. Are your parents with you? Your husband/wife to be is at your side. How does he/she look? Happy? Notice the beautiful flowers on the temple grounds. It's the early morning of a beautiful sunny day. You and your loved one walk hand in hand into the temple. The person at the desk asks for your temple recommend. How do you feel knowing that you are worthy to enter the house of the Lord?

Being married in the temple means you never gave up on yourself. It means you are willing to make God a partner in your marriage. It means you want to fulfill your life's mission. It means you and your spouse will work to make your relationship stay strong. It means your children will have a father who gives them priesthood blessings when they're sick, and a mother who loves and nurtures them. It means that when problems come, you'll work together to overcome them.

Now pick one of your most important goals and imagine yourself achieving it. Run it like a movie in your mind when you get discouraged. If John Goddard can accomplish his goals, you can accomplish yours. I know you can do it.

CHAPTER SEVEN

Making Your Dreams Come True

This is a scene from *Home Cooking on the Wasatch Range*, a play of mine produced at BYU in 1980 under the direction of Kaye Hansen. In this scene Tony, a transfer student at BYU from New Jersey, tries to help Cher, who is from New York, set goals that will cause his roommate BJ to propose to her.

Cher finishes cleaning up the kitchen, hangs up her apron and sits down beside Tony, who has been writing at the kitchen table.

TONY: (Referring to paper.) I've made a list of things a guy looks for in an LDS girl. I thought we'd go over 'em and maybe pick out some goals. Okay?

CHER: (Shrugs her shoulders.) Yeah.

TONY: I listed testimony first.

CHER: I've got one. I really do.

TONY: Fine. I'll check that one. (Marks paper.) The next one I listed is body.

CHER: That didn't take long, did it?

TONY: Now you can break the body down to face, and then figure. First is face.

CHER: I don't know . . . What do you think?

TONY: Hmm . . . (Moves aside her hair to look at her neck.) You got a neck and ears. That's good . . . overall, I'd say it's a good face.

CHER: Except for the glasses.

TONY: You gotta see.

CHER: I'll get contact lenses.

TONY: I like you the way you are.

CHER: It's not you I'm trying to please though.

TONY: Right. (Writes.) Next we have figure. (Cher stands up and slowly turns around. Tony clears his throat.)

CHER: Well?

TONY: It's fine.

CHER: (Facing him.) It's not the greatest . . .

TONY: Don't worry about it. I think you're great. The next one on the list is common interests. Since BJ's biggest interest is BJ, at least you've got that in common.

CHER: Tony, be constructive.

TONY: Okay. Let's see, common interests. Guys from the West are crazy about killing deer. Do you know anything about that?

CHER: What's there to know?

TONY: Well, do you know how to clean a deer?

CHER: Do they get dirty?

TONY: That brings us to the next one on the list, a sense of humor.

CHER: I'm not sure BJ has one.

TONY: For you, being married to him'd be a joke.

CHER: What's the next one?

TONY: A supporting attitude . . . like cooking his favorite foods. What does he like?

CHER: He likes dry, black, crusty burnt pot roast. It's like a burnt offering. Okay, I'll start burning his food for him. (Tony writes that down.)

TONY: That's all I have on my list. By all counts you oughta be married.

CHER: There must be more. Maybe I should do things that other Mormon girls do, like learning to dry apricot pits. I know, I still have some of my Eastern cynicism. I need to be sincere and say things like, "Today is the first day of the rest of my life." (Tony writes it down.)

Notice that in this scene Cher and Tony set some goals and wrote them down. It's a good practice to get into.

I learned about goal setting as a bishop. Every time I was about to do a youth interview, our Young Women's president would say, "Be sure and talk to them about their goals." And so I would, at first just because she said so.

Oh sure, I thought it was a good idea for youth to set goals, but I wasn't that fired up about it for myself. But the more I sold it to the youth, the more it became a part of my life too.

You may recall my decision to write *Charly* began

with a written goal. I wrote the goal in my journal and then on a three-by-five card that I taped on the inside of my desk drawer so I'd see it every day. Having a written goal helped me get it done. And since *Charly* changed my life, I'm recommending goal setting to you.

Here are the nuts and bolts of goal setting:

1. Daydream.

2. Write down everything you want to happen in your life.

3. List your goals in order of importance to you. Weed out goals that might conflict with each other.

4. Go over the list and rewrite your goals so they are specific and have a definite deadline for completion.

5. Take the most important long-range goals and turn them into a series of short-range goals.

Let's go over these one at a time.

1. *Daydream.* We've done a little of this already. If you could be anything in the world, what would it be? What kind of person do you want to become?

This is the beginning for everything else. Unless you can get a picture in your mind of the good things you want to happen in your life, they may never happen to you.

2. *Write down everything you want to happen in your life.* You've already done this, right?

3. *List your goals in order of importance to you. Weed out goals that might conflict with each other.*

Suppose one of your goals is to be a brain surgeon and another one is to be president of the United States. Can you see there might be a conflict between these two goals? There have been very few brain surgeon presidents in United States history. So you might have to decide between the two. Would you rather be a brain surgeon or the president of the United States?

Maybe you have a goal to own a Corvette by the time you're twenty-two years old and also a goal to go on a mission as soon as possible. For most people this would be unrealistic.

4. *Rewrite your goals so they are specific and have a definite deadline for completion.*

The problem with a goal like, "I'll become a better person," is that it's difficult to measure. Nobody has invented a better-person meter to find out if your better-person measurement has gone from 3.6 to 4.2.

In contrast you can measure a goal like, "I will do ten sit-ups a day from now until Christmas." At the end of each day, you either have or you haven't done ten sit-ups.

A deadline for achievement is also crucial to goal setting. When I set a goal to write *Charly*, I said I'd send a manuscript to a publisher by a specific date. If I'd left out the deadline, maybe I'd still be writing it.

Here are some examples of specific goals with deadlines.

A. For the next month I will read five pages a day in the New Testament.

B. I will go out for track this spring.

C. For the next month, once a day, I will talk to someone at school who usually gets ignored by others.

D. Within the next month I will learn what colors I look good in. After I find out, I will buy a sweater or shirt in one of these colors.

E. Once a week I will have a long talk (10 minutes or more) with my parents.

F. At least once a day, I'll pray.

G. This summer I'll take tennis lessons.

H. This Saturday I will write a song.

All of these goals are specific and have definite deadlines for accomplishment.

5. *Take your most important long-range goals and turn each one into a series of short-range goals.*

Very few worthwhile things in life just happen.

There's the old joke that the way to eat an elephant is one bite at a time. This is the same idea. What you do is "chunk" your most important goals into monthly, then weekly, and finally daily goals.

Let's take an example. Suppose you are 16 years old and you decide you want to be a physician. We first break this into year-sized chunks. The process might end up something like this:

Age	Goals	Check if Accomplished
16	• Take Biology I.	☐
	• Take Chemistry.	☐
	• Take Algebra.	☐
17	• Take Biology II.	☐
	• Take Physics.	☐
	• Take Geometry.	☐
	• Ask a doctor for advice.	☐
	• Read *The Memory Book*.	☐
	• Memorize names of all the bones in the human body.	☐
	• Find out which colleges have the greatest percentage of premed graduates admitted to medical school.	☐
18	• Take the SAT or ACT exam.	☐
	• Graduate from high school.	☐
	• Enroll as freshman in premed.	☐
	• Get at least a 3.5 GPA.	☐
19-21	• Serve a mission (it will be later if you're female).	☐

You may think a mission will slow you down professionally. Okay, you're right, it may do that. If it does, then that makes it a real sacrifice, doesn't it? It's your gift to Heavenly Father for all the things he's done for you.

But on the other hand, a mission may not slow you down at all. In fact it may pay dividends for the rest of your life. A mission is excellent preparation for success in any field. After you return from your mission, you'll have more maturity and wisdom than others your age. In addition, you will have learned how to work, how to manage time, and more important, you will have developed great faith in your Father in Heaven.

If I had to choose between the eight years I spent in college or the two years I spent on a mission, I would still choose to go on a mission. It was a valuable experience for me.

We could of course continue the list of yearly goals on the road to becoming a physician, but by now you probably see how such a list could be put together.

Let's suppose you've prepared a list of yearly goals. Now what do you do? You take the yearly goals for this year and break them up into monthly goals.

For example, suppose you're seventeen and have chosen yearly goals to help you become a physician. This is the way the yearly goals might look if they were broken up into monthly goals. We'll begin with September.

Month	Goal	Check
September	• Check out *The Memory Book* from library.	☐
	• Read one hundred pages of *The Memory Book*.	☐
	• Enroll in Biology I.	☐
	• Enroll in Geometry.	☐

- Enroll in Physics. ☐
- Go out for cross-country. ☐
- Learn to cook a pot roast. ☐
- Talk parents into buying a VCR for Halloween. ☐

October
- Finish *The Memory Book*. ☐
- Go out for the school play. ☐
- Learn to play one song on the piano. ☐
- Talk parents into buying a VCR for Thanksgiving. ☐
- Check out from library a book that tells what colors are good for me. Read it. ☐
- Phone a doctor and ask if I can come and talk to her. Ask her for advice. ☐

November
- Memorize a *Time* magazine. Bring it to school. ☐
- Play my one piano song for my next date. ☐
- Talk parents into buying a VCR for Christmas. ☐
- Phone a brain surgeon and ask for an appointment (for advice not for treatment). ☐

And so forth. Now what? You take the monthly goals and break them into weekly goals.

And then what? You take the weekly goals and break them into daily goals.

Let me show you what daily goals could look like.

Day	Goal	Check
Monday, November 3	• Tell parents that if we had a VCR, we could watch LDS conference tapes every Sunday.	☐
	• Have Mom show me how to play second line of the song *Tomorrow*.	☐
	• Study for Biology exam.	☐
	• Dissect my guinea pig at home. Be sure and announce to the rest of my family I've put it in refrigerator and they should leave it alone.	☐

The idea is simple: if you do the daily goals, then you automatically accomplish the weekly goals. If you attain your weekly goals, then you'll succeed at the monthly goals. If you achieve the monthly goals, then you'll reach your yearly goals. If you complete your yearly goals, then you'll make your five-year goals. And so forth on to eternity.

Does it work? Yes, of course. Why not try it?

Homework

Take one of your most important goals and break it down into shorter-term goals. Then set yearly, monthly, weekly, and finally daily goals.

CHAPTER EIGHT

The Other Side of the Coin

My parents were pleased I was dating again and had forgotten about Charly. The trouble was, I hadn't.

I was miserable—a man dying of thirst in the middle of a fresh-water lake. . . .

One girl I spent a lot of time with was Kay Randall. We both were studying computer science, and had several classes together. In November, feeling guilty about never having asked her out, I invited her to a movie.

"Let's say you take the worst possible case," she droned on over a piece of pie in a restaurant off-campus after the movie. "Suppose you have a loss-of-cooling accident. What should you do?"

"What?" I asked.

"Aren't you listening?"

"No, you're really boring me," I confessed.

"I thought you'd appreciate my [computer] program."

"How about if we go to the airport at Salt Lake and pretend that you've just gotten off a plane from Yugoslavia, can't speak a word of English, and I'm your boyfriend."

"That's a long way to drive for a kiss."

"I don't want to kiss you—I just want some excitement."

"Thanks a lot," she good-naturedly frowned.

"Or how about if we go to a Chinese restaurant and pretend we're spies, and pass secret notes to each other?"

"That sounds really juvenile to me."

"Right—let's be juvenile."

"Why?"

"I'm tired of being mature. It's no fun. Kay, let me ask you a personal question. OK?"

"Well, I guess so."

"Do you have a things-to-do list?"

"That's a personal question? Yes."

"Me, too. And every morning do you write down what you want to accomplish that day, then when you've done it, you check it off the list?"

"Sure, I do that."

"Isn't that terrible?" I groaned.

"I don't see anything terrible about it."

"Don't you? It's ruining our lives." I pulled out my three-by-five card from my shirt pocket. "Here's mine today. 'Do laundry. Put on snow tires. Take Kay out.' At the end of our date, I'm going to put a check beside 'Take Kay out.'"

"So?"

"So you're just one more on the list with dirty clothes and bald tires." (From the novel *Charly*.)

We've talked about goal-setting. Now I need to give you a caution. Goal setting, carried to the extreme, can be a monster.

What happens to a goal-setter who gets up in the morning, writes out a list of things to do for the day, and then comes across a friend in desperate need of help. What does a goal-setter do then? Throw away the list and show some compassion, right? That's what should be done. But it's not always what a dedicated goal-setter will do.

In the parable of the Good Samaritan, you'll recall the two travelers who pass a wounded man without giving any assistance at all. I wonder if they had in their hand an Old Testament version of a things-to-do list.

In your drive to achieve goals, don't lose your compassion. Sometimes it's more important to help a friend in need than it is to accomplish your goal of twenty-five push-ups. When in doubt, ask yourself what the Savior would do in a similar situation.

A small confession—I need to be less concerned about pursuing goals when sensitivity and compassion are needed. I'm working on it. In fact it's one of my new goals.

As long as we're advising caution, let's talk about perfection. In our church we often quote "Be ye therefore perfect, even as your Father which is in Heaven is perfect." (Matthew 5:48.)

It's possible to have misconceptions about what was intended in this counsel from the Savior. Let me list a few.

1. *Some people think being perfect means never making any mistakes.*

And yet, when you're learning a new skill, you have to make mistakes. It's the only way to learn.

The scriptures tell us that Joseph was a carpenter. I imagine that while Jesus was young, Joseph must have taught him a few carpentry skills. Do you suppose that, as as boy, Jesus never made an error in measuring or fitting a piece of wood? I think he did. Then how can we say he was perfect? Because he was always true to Father in Heaven.

We must never be afraid of making the kind of mistakes that are necessary in order to learn.

2. *Some things are not worth the effort perfection would take.*

Sometimes we make the mistake of paying first-class devotion to a second-class cause. For example, everyone should have at least one cluttered drawer. Why? Because it's too much trouble to keep everything in perfect order.

Here's another example. A teenage girl may get into a dangerous cycle while trying to lose weight. At first she just doesn't want to be overweight. But if she loses weight, then she may set a new goal to be five pounds under-weight, and then fifteen, and on and on. This kind of self-destructive goal setting can lead to severe problems, such as bulimia or anorexia, which may eventually cause death.

Guys can get on this kick too. They can become compulsive weightlifters, spending hours and hours pumping iron and looking at their muscles in a mirror, hoping to reach that perfect form.

Let's be realistic. Suppose you had a perfect body, what on earth would you do with it? Let's imagine that after months of exercising you finally achieve the perfect body at 2:36 P.M. on a Wednesday afternoon. You run over to your best friend's house, enthusiastically knock on the door, and when your friend answers you say, "Hey! Look at me! I have a perfect body!"

Your friend yawns, lets you in, and says, "Yeah, it's nice."

"No, you don't understand. My body is perfect. Look at my forearm. Look at my stomach muscles. Have you ever seen such a marvelous stomach? There's not an ounce of fat on it. I'm so happy! You don't know how hard I've worked on my stomach."

Your friend says, "Yeah, well I was wondering why you never do things with us anymore like you used to."

"Hey, let's show a little appreciation here. This is a perfect body! Look at my calf muscles. Look what they do when I stand up. See how they ripple? And look at my deltoids! Have you ever seen deltoids like this before? Some day I'll be in the Deltoid Hall of Fame."

Your friend says, "Yeah, they're real nice. Hey, do you want some cookies? My mom just made some."

You cringe. "Eat cookies? Are you serious? What are you trying to do, tear down what I've spent the last six months working on? I can't eat cookies."

"Why not?"

After a long pause, you finally admit it. "If I ate a cookie, then my body wouldn't be perfect anymore."

Your friend looks at you strangely. "Just one cookie would do that?"

"Of course. You have no idea what one cookie can do to a perfect body like mine."

"Oh," your friend says slowly. "Well, what are you going to do now that your body is perfect?"

You wait a long time before answering. "I can't quit now. I've got to keep on my schedule. Sure, my body's perfect now. But what about tomorrow? What if I gain an ounce? That'd be awful. What if my stomach muscles sag? What if I wake up in the morning five pounds heavier than I am now? I'd better go now. I need to go home and do my deltoid exercises."

Can you see that a goal to have a perfect body would put you on a never-ending treadmill? You'd end up spending your life on bathroom scales, scowling critically at yourself in front of a mirror. You would be ever turning inward instead of focusing your attention outward to those who need what only you can give them—yourself.

How important is it to have a perfect body? If your best friend gained five pounds, would you end your friendship? If you gained five pounds, would any of your friends drop you? Of course not.

It is estimated that over twenty-five percent of women and teenage girls have some form of eating disorder. They overeat or don't eat at all.

It's not hard to see why compulsive behavior about food exists these days. Look at the TV ads. First they tell us to eat a Snickers candy bar and then they tell us we're too fat and need to go on a diet. There's a food war going on in our living rooms, and we are the casualties.

The entire nation is on a diet. Let's face facts. Not every girl in America can look like a model. And not every guy can look like Arnold Schwarzenegger.

We're people, not statues. Statues can have perfect bodies that never change with time. But people are so much more fun to be around than statues. People make jokes and grin and get freckles in the summer and do cartwheels on the lawn. But statues are cold and hard and uncaring. I'd rather be a person with a real live lumpy body than a cold hard perfect statue.

If weight is a problem to you I recommend a book called *How to Lower Your Fat Thermostat*, by Dr. Garth Fisher and Dr. Dennis Remington. Basically it says that if you want to lose weight, whatever you do, don't go on a diet, because diets will cause you to gain weight.

How can a diet cause you to gain weight? It's very simple. You go on a diet and your stomach yells out, "Hey, what's going on here? Where's the food?"

Your mind says, "We've decided to cut down."

"Are you crazy?" your stomach complains. "What am I supposed to do down here with less food coming in?"

"Get used to it."

You start to lose weight in the first few days of your diet, but then your stomach decides it had better get more efficient, so it begins to wring out every possible bit of energy it can from the tiny morsels of food you send it each day.

Because your stomach has become more efficient, you stop losing weight even though you're only eating just a tiny bit of food each day. Also, the body shuts down; you don't have as much energy as you used to have.

Eventually you can't stand it and you go off your diet. Let's take the day you go off your diet. Suddenly you're eating chocolate sundaes and hamburgers and fries and root beer. But, because of your diet, your digestive system is still very efficient, and since there's more than enough energy there for a day, it begins storing the rest in the form of fat cells.

So after you go off your diet, you gain weight because your body was forced to become more efficient because you went on a diet. In other words, your diet has caused you to gain weight! And after five years of on-again, off-again dieting, you'll end up weighing more than if you'd never dieted at all.

Listen to what Garth Fisher said in an interview in *This People* magazine: "One woman told me she'd tried every diet known to man, and that her weight had yo-yo'd up and down the scale most of her life. At my encouragement she gave up her diet, and now she's lost sixty-five pounds."

So what's the best way to lose weight? That's covered in *How to Lower Your Fat Thermostat* too. Let me give you a quick summary. What you need to do is fool your stomach into thinking there's plenty of food coming in, so there's no use being very efficient. Oddly enough if you want to lose weight, you need to eat well. Seems strange, doesn't it?

The foods you should eat to lose weight are fresh vegetables and fruits, rice, whole-wheat bread and cereal, soups, and lean cuts of meat. Cut down on hamburgers, french fries, soft drinks, pizza, ice cream, cookies, cake, and candy.

It's a bitter pill to swallow, isn't it? If you want to lose weight, you have to eat the foods your mother has been telling you to eat. "Eat your vegetables. Have some oatmeal. You're not eating your carrots. Have some more squash. If you're hungry, eat an apple."

Another important factor in weight control is to get involved in a daily aerobic exercise program, such as jogging, swimming, taking long walks, or aerobic dancing. (With your doctor's approval of course.)

Have you ever seen a fat zebra? Or a chubby deer? Why not? Because they eat their vegetables and grains and they get a lot of exercise. So it must work, right? I mean, how many deer go on diets?

As you mature you eventually realize there's so many other things in life to think about that you shouldn't waste time worrying about having a perfect body. Every person reaches the point where he or she thinks, "Hey, I can live with this body. So maybe it's not the greatest in the world, but it isn't the worst either. It's got some nice things going for it. Besides, the people who really count in my life like me the way I am. And the rest, well, they don't count that much anyway. I can live with things the way they are."

3. *Some people think they have to be Little Ms. Perfect or Never Ruffled Mr. Perfect.*

Some people think you should never show anger. I wonder why they think that. The Savior showed anger. You always knew what he was thinking. Sometimes he got really mad at his disciples. And when he did, he let them know.

For example, in Matthew 16:16 Peter bears his testimony that Jesus is the Christ, the son of the living God.

In verse seventeen, Jesus says to Peter, "Blessed art

thou, Simon Bar-jona: for flesh and blood hath not revealed it unto thee, but my Father which is heaven."

In verse twenty-one, Jesus foretells his death and resurrection.

In verse twenty-two it says: "Then Peter took him, and began to rebuke him, saying, Be it far from thee, Lord: this shall not be unto thee."

In verse twenty-three, Jesus rebuked Peter: "Get thee behind me, Satan: thou art an offence unto me: for thou savourest not the things that be of God, but those that be of men."

In other words, Jesus was honest when he felt the need to communicate his emotions. Does anyone think he can improve on the Savior's example?

Little Ms. Perfect always tries to be "nice." Even when she doesn't feel good. And so she puts up a front of always being in control. Never Ruffled Mr. Perfect pretends he's above emotion, that logic and reason govern his every move.

An example of this can be found in my book *Sam*.

In church we were model newlyweds. Bright, cheerful in a crowd, we both tried desperately to find safe, trivial topics when we were alone.

We attended a Sunday School class in family relations. One day the bishop came to talk to the class.

"Most of the problems in a marriage revolve around poor communication. Much of the time I find the wife wants to come in for counseling, but her husband won't admit there's a problem."

On the way home, Lara asked, "What would you think about our going to the bishop?"

"What for?" I asked.

"Our problems."

"What problems?" I snickered. "We don't have any problems. We don't even argue."

"We never talk anymore."

"We're talking now."

"Sam, just tell me what's wrong. Is it something I'm doing wrong?"

"There's nothing wrong."

It's all right to have feelings. It's all right to get mad, discouraged, happy, silly, or worried. These are feelings. You can't be talked out of how you feel by someone saying, "You shouldn't feel that way."

Sometimes you need to express your feelings, especially if you're mad. The Savior did, so we can too. Here are some ground rules that may help you express your feelings.

First of all, try to avoid "you" messages. Some examples of "you" messages are, *"You* are the biggest idiot I've ever seen!" or "Can't *you* do anything right?"

In communicating feelings, try to give "I" messages. An "I" message tells how you feel because of what happened. Avoid placing blame where possible. Here are some examples: "I'm mad because I had to wait here for an hour" or "I'm furious when someone eats my share of dessert."

The Savior gave good counsel about expressing feelings. "Reproving betimes with sharpness, when moved upon by the Holy Ghost; and then showing forth afterwards an increase of love toward him whom thou hast reproved, lest he esteem thee to be his enemy." (D&C 121:43.)

4. *Some people think of perfection as if it were to be achieved by checking all the squares on a checklist.*

But the list keeps getting longer and longer as time goes on, and nobody around these people can ever stack up to their expectations.

If you have ever watched the TV show "St. Elsewhere," you'll remember Dr. Craig, chief of surgeons. He never says anything nice about the people he works with. Why not? Because he has a mile-long list of desirable traits he wants in a coworker, and nobody but himself can live up to those standards.

Sometimes, if we're not careful, we can become like that.

Of course there are some things we need to do to inherit the celestial kingdom. We need to live the commandments. We need to receive certain ordinances such as baptism and temple endowments. We need to live righteously. We need to follow counsel from our leaders.

But some people, after they've run out of basic commandments, create their own list. And as soon as all the items on the list are checked off, they make an even longer list.

So what's wrong with that? Maybe nothing. Except a person like this is often very critical of others because they are not living up to every item on the list. This can cause problems for family and friends, because no matter how well they live, they're made to feel they just don't measure up to what's expected.

The problem with these never-ending checklists is that they may cause us to miss out on what our main purpose in life should be. In 1965, President David O. McKay made the following statement to a group of Church employees:

"Let me assure you, Brethren, that some day you will have a personal interview with the Savior himself. If you are interested, I will tell you the order in which he will ask you to account for your earthly responsibilities.

"First, he will request an accountability report about your relationship with your wife. Have you actively been engaged in making her happy and ensuring that her needs have been met as an individual?

"Second, he will want an accountability report about each of your children individually. He will not attempt to have this for simply a family stewardship but will request information about your relationship to each and every child.

"Third, he will want to know what you personally have done with talents you were given in the preexistence.

"Fourth, he will want a summary of your activity in your Church assignments. He will not be necessarily interested in what assignments you have had, for in his eyes the home teacher and a mission president are probably equals, but he will request a summary of how you have been of service to your fellow man in your Church assignments.

"Fifth, he will have no interest in how you earned your living but if you were honest in all your dealings.

"Sixth, he will ask for an accountability on what you have done to contribute in a positive manner to your community, state, country, and the world." (From *The Divine Center*, by Stephen R. Covey.)

What is our purpose in life? It is to become as much like the Savior as we can, in our devotion to the truth, in our obedience to divine principles, and most certainly in our love and concern for others. If we concentrate on becoming like the Savior, everything else will follow naturally.

5. *We must avoid thinking that "I'll be happy when . . ."*

This is the way we talk to ourselves sometimes. "I'd be really happy if only I were taller (or shorter), I were slimmer (or weighed more), I had more muscles in my arms, or I were smarter, or I had more hair, or I could letter in football . . ."

Be happy now with what you are and with what you have.

6. *Some people think they have two choices, either they can be perfect or else be the worst thing that ever lived.*

A person like this might start taking a class and expect perfection right away. They want an *A* on every assignment. The first exam comes along and he gets a *C*. The second exam comes along and he gets another *C*. Suddenly he decides he can't get an *A*, so he quits studying. On the next five tests, he gets an *F* and ends up flunking the course.

There's nothing wrong with a *C*. I've had my share of them. A *C* means you didn't give up. A *C* means there were a lot of people who did worse than you did. A *C* means maybe you weren't all that excited about the course, but you stuck in there and never gave up. Sometimes just getting through something is a major accomplishment.

This all-or-nothing attitude plagues people on diets. Suppose you decide to cut out sweets between meals. You do OK the first day and the second day. But on the third day, you break down and have a chocolate sundae. What do you do then? Get mad at yourself? Unleash your Bad News Coach and let him/her yell at you and tell you you'll never lose weight so why even try. Do you then go on a binge, eating sweets for a week?

No, don't do that. Just say, "Hey, it's OK, tomorrow's another day. I'll try to do better tomorrow."

What if you have a friend who's set a goal for a temple marriage, but then does something that wouldn't allow him or her to be worthy of a temple recommend. What should your friend do? Give up, quit going to church and go out and live as wild a life as possible?

I hope a person in this situation would have enough faith in the Savior to know that forgiveness is possible if he or she will go through the repentance process. It's not easy, but it is possible.

Don't give up on your dreams. Don't quit. Take one day at a time. Do the best you can.

If you can't be an A student today, then be a C student. But be a C student who's trying to become a C+ student. And when you reach that, then be a C+ student who's trying to become a B student. Don't set impossible goals and then cave-in when you don't reach them. We will exist forever, so we've got enough time to perfect any talent if we just hang in there and don't give up.

Never give up. Never write yourself off. Never say it doesn't matter anymore what you do. Never think that you've gone too far to be able to make things right again. Never quit trying.

7. *Some people think that perfection has to be achieved today.*

We gain perfection by improving a little each year.

Here is an example that makes the law of eternal progression understandable. It was first proposed by Dr. John H. Gardner of Brigham Young University.

Suppose you deposit $100 in the bank. The bank will give you six percent interest compounded annually. How much will you have at the end of each year?

After one year you will have gained six percent of $100, or $6. After two years you will gain six percent of $106, or $6.36. Then your total will be $112.36.

Pay attention to the 36 cents. That's six percent of the $6 earned as interest the year before—36 lousy cents. Who could imagine that it would ever amount to anything. But wait a few years. Each year you gain six percent of what you had at the beginning of that year.

It doesn't seem you'll ever make much money doing this, but let's just see what your balance is as the years go on.

Number of Years	Balance in Dollars
1	106
5	134
10	179
20	321
30	574
50	1,842
100	33,930
150	625,000
200	11,512,590
250	212,063,691
300	3,906,245,905
350	71,953,000,000
400	1,325,400,000,000
500	449,710,000,000,000

And that's just after five hundred years! But we're going to live forever, so if we can get a little better each year, eventually we'll become millions of times better than we are right now.

That's where perfection takes place—over the long run, not next week.

Right now our big hurdle is this earth life. If we can prove true and faithful, there's no limit to the growth we can experience over the thousands of years that will follow.

So don't worry about becoming perfect over night. Live the commandments, try to learn new skills, develop your God-given talents, center your life as much as you can on the Savior, and just keep plugging away.

Homework

William James said, "The art of becoming wise is the art of knowing what to overlook."

Which of the following can sometimes be sluffed off?

1. Having a clean room
2. Doing your homework
3. Being polite
4. Talking with a soft voice
5. Getting good grades
6. Doing what you're asked to do
7. Attending church

The truth is there are times when you can sluff off any of these. When you're sick, or you need to rest. That might mean your homework won't get done. Sometimes instead of studying, you may need to comfort a friend. If your stomach is churning with pent-up feelings of anger, you need to find a way to let it out, even if it means yelling. If you're about to be kidnapped, you no longer have to be polite and do what you're asked. You can yell and scream to get people to realize what's happening. If you've been the victim of sexual abuse, you need to tell someone about it even if the person abusing you has warned you to keep quiet. Attending church is important, but if some weekend someone in the family is very sick and needs you to take care of them, then that may be the most important thing for you to do.

Maturity involves being able to decide, "What's the best thing for me to do now?"

"Now it came to pass, as they went, that he entered

into a certain village: and a certain woman named Martha received him into her house. And she had a sister Mary, which also sat at Jesus' feet, and heard his word. But Martha was cumbered about much serving, and came to him, and said, Lord, dost thou not care that my sister hath left me to serve alone? Bid her therefore that she help me. And Jesus answered and said unto her, Martha, Martha, thou art careful and troubled about many things: But one thing is needful: and Mary hath chosen that good part, which shall not be taken away from her." (Luke 10:39-42.)

Of course Mary knew she should help her sister prepare the meal, but she also realized that she was in the company of the Messiah. She wanted to be able to spend as much time as she could with him. And so she chose not to help.

She couldn't use that as an excuse everytime they had guests, but in that instance the best thing for her to do was to be near Jesus and talk to him. She had to choose her priorities—just as you will throughout your life. I hope you will, as Mary did, choose the good part.

CHAPTER NINE

The Land of Beginning Again

I wish that there were some wonderful place
    Called the Land of Beginning Again,
Where all our mistakes and all our heartaches
    And all of our poor selfish grief
Could be dropped like a shabby old coat at the door,
    And never be put on again.
                —Louise Fletcher

Some mistakes in life are more serious than missing a thrown ball or muffing a note on the piano. They're the kind of mistakes we call sin.

We've all sinned. It's a fact of human existence. So it's important to know how to deal with it, how to repent, and how to take advantage of the Savior's atonement to relieve us of the burdens of sin.

Our Bad News Coach has a field day when we've committed a serious sin. He begins shouting in our face, "You've really done it now. What were you thinking of? I hope you know there's no way you're ever going to be forgiven of this. It's all over. How could you be so stupid? How could you have done anything so dumb? And you call yourself a member of the Church? Do you know what your friends would say if they knew about this? You think they'd even want you in the same room? Forget it. You might just as well give up now because God's written you off."

Your Bad News Coach would like you to believe that because you've made one mistake it's all over, there's no hope for you, and you might as well quit trying.

Would you like to know what the Lord says? "Behold, he who has repented of his sins, the same is forgiven, and I, the Lord, remember them no more. By this ye may know if a man repenteth of his sins—behold, he will confess them and forsake them." (D&C 58:42-43.)

This means we can start over again. There *is* a Land of Beginning Again.

President Harold B. Lee once observed: "If the time comes when you have done all that you can do to repent of your sins, whoever you are, wherever you are, and you have made amends and restitution to the best of your ability; if it be something that will affect your standing in the Church and you have gone to the proper authorities, then you will want that confirming answer as to whether or not the Lord has accepted of you. In your soul-searching, if you seek for and you find that peace of conscience, by that token you may know that he Lord has accepted of your repentance. *Satan would have you think otherwise and sometimes persuade you that now having made one mistake, you might go on and on with no turning back. That is one of the great falsehoods. The miracle of forgiveness is available to all of those who turn from their evil doings and return no more, because the Lord has said in a revelation to us in our day: 'go your way and sin no more; but unto that soul who sinneth [meaning again] shall the former sins return, saith the Lord your God.'* (D&C 82:7.)" (Italics added.)

So it's possible to start over, to begin again. How do we do it? Here are the steps of repentance.

1. We need to feel bad about what we've done.
2. We need to decide to change our lives.

3. We need to decide where to start.
4. We need to confess our sins.
5. We need to make restitution.
6. We need to take steps so that similar problems won't recur.
7. We need to put our trust in the Savior.
8. Once repentance is complete, we need to forgive ourselves and not dwell on past mistakes.

We'll go over these one at a time.

1. *We need to feel bad about what we've done.*

Feeling guilty is a gift from God. It's designed to prompt us to change our life. If we feel bad about having done something wrong, in a way that's good, because it means we're still basically good. If we didn't feel guilty, things would be far worse.

2. *We need to decide to change our life.*

Guilt is a terrible burden. It brings torment, misery, and gloom and robs us of our self-confidence.

God never intended for us to carry guilt around with us for the rest of our lives. It's purpose is to cause us to repent. As soon as we complete the repentance process, the need for guilt is gone. It should be swept away, leaving us feeling clean and optimistic again. "And I also thank God, Yea, my great God, that he hath granted unto us that we might repent of these things, and also that he hath forgiven us of those our many sins . . . and *taken away the guilt from our hearts, through the merits of his Son.*" (Alma 24:10; italics added.)

That's the way it's supposed to work. Guilt is the catalyst for change.

3. *We need to decide where to start in improving our lives.*

President Harold B. Lee said this: "What is the most

important of all the commandments of the gospel? If you will think about that rather carefully and thoughtfully, you will see that the most important of all the commandments for you at this moment is the one you are having the most difficulty keeping. If it's dishonesty, that's your problem, and yours is the task to overcome dishonesty. If it's falsehood, if it's betrayal of your friends, if it's unchastity, today is the day for you to consider that as the most important of all the commandments of the gospel of Jesus Christ. And when you have successfully mastered that particular problem, then you should select the next one you are having trouble with and so on until you have conquered them all."

4. *We need to confess our sins.*

Who are the ones we should confess our sins to? First of all, Father in Heaven. We need to pray and tell him what we've done and ask for his forgiveness.

We also need to confess and apologize to the person we've wronged.

We may wish to tell our parents so they can help us through the difficult times ahead.

In some cases, we should tell our bishop or branch president. Sins involving sexual misconduct or dishonesty are some of the sins that should be talked over with our bishop.

I've been a bishop. Can I tell you what it's like to hear someone's confession? It's much different than you might think. There's a gift that goes with being a bishop. I knew when I had it, and I felt it leave when I was released. It allowed me to focus on what the Savior would focus on—true repentance. It allowed me to separate the sin from the sinner. That is, even if the sin is awful, the person is not. A bishop's main goal is to get a person to become eligible to take advantage of the Savior's atonement.

And so if you need to, talk to your bishop. Even though I don't know who he is, I trust Heavenly Father will help him know what to do for you.

We can be forgiven. We can start over again. Isn't that terrific?

Here's another scene from *Charly*. It happens just after Charly's baptism.

Charly and I sat, both wearing jeans, barefoot in the middle of my parents' garden. We had been weeding but were taking a rest, facing away from each other, my back propped against hers, with our bare feet planted in the warm, dark soil. The cornstalks towered over our heads, and we heard the hum of bees, while overhead small, puffy clouds paraded by. I liked that lusty smell from the nearby tomato plants and the feel of her warm back against mine and the combined smells of her perspiration and shampoo.

"Nice going, Earth. Nice going, Father in Heaven," she purred.

She moved around and sat in front of me.

"Sam, I've never felt so clean in my life."

"Oh yeah?" I smiled. "Well, your feet are dirty."

"Sure, but that will wash off. I meant a different kind of clean. Is it true that when I was baptized all my past sins were washed away and I started off with a clean slate?"

"That's right."

"And you believe that?"

"Sure. I taught it for two years on my mission."

"So, right now, I'm as pure and clean as any other girl in the ward?"

"Except for your feet, sure. Why do you ask?"

"I just wanted to be sure I understood. And Heavenly Father will forget any bad I did before my baptism?"

"He'll forget the things we repent of."

"Isn't that terrific?" she beamed. "What a nice thing to do for us."

"I agree."

"But what about you? What about your sins? It's been a long time since you were baptized."

"I have to keep repenting. That's one of the reasons we take the sacrament each Sunday: so we can renew the covenants of baptism."

5. *We need to make restitution.*

If we've stolen something, then we need to give it back. If we've told rumors about people, we need to go back and tell the truth.

Here is what President Joseph F. Smith said: "True repentance is not only sorrow for sins and humble penitence and contrition before God, but it involves the necessity of turning away from them, a discontinuance of all evil practices and deeds, a thorough reformation of life, a vital change from evil to good, from vice to virtue, from darkness to light. Not only so, but to make restitution, so far as it is possible, for all the wrongs we have done, to pay our debts, and restore to God and man their rights—that which is due them from us. This is true repentance, and the exercise of the will and all the powers of mind and body is demanded, to complete this glorious work of repentance."

6. *We need to take steps so that similar problems won't recur.*

Suppose that whenever I go into a bakery, I steal a doughnut. Other than that I'm very honest. What should I do to keep from stealing doughnuts? Sure—stay away from the bakery.

Suppose I have a friend who has a VCR at home and likes to invite friends over on weekends to watch R-rated movies? Suppose I've been going for the past few weeks, but now my conscience is beginning to bother me because of what I've been seeing. What would be a good first step? Of course—quit going to my friend's house on Friday nights.

Here's a scene from the play *Home Cooking on the Wasatch Range*. This scene involves Brad, a shy physics graduate student, and Jenny, a vivacious blonde athlete.

BRAD: The more we kiss, the more of a problem it is for me. . . . Jenny, we've got a problem. . . . When we're apart, I'm miserable. And now lately when we're together, I'm miserable too, but in a different way. (They sit down, at opposite ends of the couch.)

JENNY: So what are we going to do?

BRAD: I should know. We had so many lessons on this in priests quorum. Our adviser even had us carry a set of rules in our wallets. (Goes for his wallet.) Want to hear 'em?

JENNY: I always wondered what guys talked about in priesthood meeting.

BRAD: Rule number one: "Never be alone in a room with a member of the opposite sex." (They look warily around the room.)

BRAD: Let's get out of here. We'll wait outside 'til Tony gets home.

JENNY: But it's snowing outside. (Helps her on with her coat, then puts his on.)

BRAD: (Reading.) Rule number two: "When temptation comes, run three miles a day."

JENNY: So that's why so many guys jog.

BRAD: Rule number three: "When you're tempted, sing a church hymn." (As they exit, Brad begins to quietly sing a church hymn.)

As Jenny and Brad demonstrate, we need to have guidelines that will help us avoid the situations that lead to immorality.

7. *We need to put our trust in the Savior.*
"Now this is the commandment: Repent, all ye ends of the earth, and come unto me and be baptized in my name, that ye may be sanctified by the reception of the Holy Ghost, that ye may stand spotless before me at the last day." (3 Nephi 27:20.)

"Behold, he who has repented of his sins, the same is forgiven, and I, the Lord, remember them no more." (D&C 58:42.)

We can always count on the Savior to do his part if we will do our part.

8. *Once repentance is complete, we need to forgive ourselves and not dwell on past mistakes.*
If God, the purest of all, can forgive us of our sins, if he can even forget the transgressions we've repented of, then we should forgive ourselves too.

If we've gone through the steps of repentance, then we shouldn't let our Bad News Coach use our past sins to depress us. If we used to steal things but we don't anymore, then we must not allow our Bad News Coach to call us "thief" for the rest of our lives.

Past sins are like garbage. Once truly repented of, they should be carted off to the dump and forgotten and never brought back or repeated.

Let's close with this scene from *Charly.*

She took a deep breath and closed her eyes. "Sam, before I joined the Church, or even knew anything about it, there were some problems in my life, problems that would've prevented me from getting a temple recommend if I'd been a member of the Church. I thought I should tell you."

"What kind of problems?"

She pursed her lips. "Problems of moral cleanliness."

I felt sick.

. . . "Sam, it was before I even had heard about the Church—in New York."

"Why didn't you tell me about this sooner?"

"When I was baptized, you told me my past sins were completely forgiven."

I couldn't let it alone. "Do you remember all their names?" I asked, tortured by my imagination.

She started to cry. "Doesn't it make any difference to you that since I've been baptized I've kept the commandments?"

"I don't want used merchandise."

I could just as well have struck her in the face—it would have hurt her less.

"I'm sorry!" I apologized, seeing the look of devastation on her face . . .

I spent the next several hours driving and thinking and, later, after my anger had subsided, praying.

Did I believe in the atonement of the Savior? Yes. Did I believe that baptism could produce a washing away of past sins? Yes. Did I believe that Charly had lived the commandments after baptism? Yes.

Then what was the problem? I could believe that the Savior could forget past sins—but I wasn't sure I could. What if I were forever haunted by bitter fantasies about her past? How could I ever forget that I, if we did get married, wasn't the first? . . .

I reflected back on the day Charly came out of the waters of baptism—the glow that filled her face. And our conversation in the garden that week after her baptism. And the changes I had seen in her as she learned about church standards. She had gradually made changes in every aspect of her life. . . . Day by day, she'd become a new person, inside and outside.

That was it! She had become a new person!

The fear and misgivings left me, and I wanted to be with her and apologize and let her know that I loved her and wasn't troubled anymore. I drove as fast as I dared down the mountain.

Homework

1. Learn more about repentance by reading and pondering about the following scriptures:
    - 3 Nephi 27:13-20
    - Alma 36:12-24
    - D&C 64:7
    - 1 John 1:9
    - Isaiah 1:18
    - D&C 18:10-13

2. Read *The Miracle of Forgiveness* by President Spencer W. Kimball.

3. Decide which of the Lord's commandments you are having the most difficulty keeping. Take advantage of Christ's atonement and go through the steps of repentance.

CHAPTER TEN

Wonder Woman Meets Superman

Heavenly Father has sent us here to grow and progress.

When we get married, suddenly we have added responsibilities, not only to ourself but to our marriage partner, and later on to our children. Things can get a little complicated at times.

In the sequel to *Charly*, Sam, after the death of his first wife Charly, marries Lara, who is in every sense a modern professional woman. At first they go through a difficult adjustment period in their marriage.

This scene occurs near the last of the book as Sam tries to sort out what the role of a man and a woman should be. He is at a park talking to his son Adam about Lara.

"A man must be strong, and his wife must be ... " I shook my head. I didn't know anymore.

A few minutes later I tried thinking out loud. "My great-grandfather—now there was a man for you. He was a pioneer with three wives when he crossed the plains. There he was, out in the wilderness, women to the right of him, women to the left of him, but he kept going. Across the wilderness they went, him at the head of his wagon, fighting the wind and the rain and the burning sun, listening to all his wives' suggestions. What a man he was, Adam. That was a time to be alive, when men were men, and women stayed in covered wagons. Now women are everywhere . . ."

"Where Mommy Rara?" Adam asked.

"Winning herself another dress. Adam, tell me something. Do you miss not having gingerbread cookies?"

"Cookie?" he asked, his eyes getting big.

"Not just any cookie—a gingerbread man with little frosting buttons and eyes and smile. I'm talking about your real, homemade gingerbread cookie. You're growing up without them. Do you miss that?"

"Adam want cookie."

"Have a donut, okay? I had gingerbread cookies when I was a boy. Your grandmother made them for me. She didn't work at a store, you know. She stayed home. When I'd come home from play, she'd give me gingerbread cookies. Adam, let me tell you, they were fun to eat. Sometimes I'd bite its little gingerbread head off in one bite."

. . . I held him in my lap and talked. "I don't really know what to tell you about being a man. Things change. A woman could be president of the United States. Think of that, Adam. Maybe a woman like Lara. She's so smart. That's my problem. I'm afraid she's better than me in every way, that she'll always have the best ideas and suggestions. What would happen to our family if I always did what she suggested? Even if she was right? Don't you see what a position I'd be placing myself in? Everyone'd think I was weak. Of course, if we always made the right decision, I guess that'd be good. Maybe it wouldn't be so bad—except I'm supposed to be the boss. How am I the boss if I always do what she suggests?"

Notice that Sam is critical of Lara because she's not making gingerbread cookies the way his own mother did. That kind of thing can cause real problems in a marriage.

A few minutes later Sam is joined by Lara. She tells

him the strain that she's felt trying to find out what he wants her to be.

"I tried," she said, "I really tried to be everything people expected me to be—a model housewife, a good cook, an efficient worker at the store, a new mother for Adam, a source of income for you so your business could get a start, a dependable person in my callings in church. I tried to do it all, and I almost made it, didn't I? Almost—I had everyone pleased, everyone but you, everyone but me. Sam, I can't be Wonder Woman anymore."

Times are changing. Traditional ideas about what roles a man or woman should fulfill are rapidly changing. You can't single-handedly fulfill every role expectation from past as well as present generations. Here's a list of what a man does. Some come from past generations. Check which ones are still a part of a man's role in today's world.

A real man—

1. harnesses up the horses when the family goes into town.
2. works in the fields all day.
3. doesn't let anyone know how worried he is.
4. is willing for his wife to develop her professional skills if she wants to.
5. fights away all intruders.
6. services his own car as well as does minor tune-ups.
7. never washes dishes, vacuums, or makes beds. That's woman's work.
8. does all the repairs in the house.
9. lays down the law with no input from his wife or children.
10. builds a house from scratch for his family.

11. never talks about his feelings.
12. lets his wife take care of raising the children while he concentrates on his career.
13. often reminds his wife that he's the boss in the family.
14. earns all the money that comes into the house.
15. is the partriarchal leader in the family.
16. always makes the final decision in everything involving the family.
17. would never allow a wife of his to get a job.
18. doesn't have to ask his wife's permission to do anything.
19. considers his wife as his first counselor in the family.

Here's a similar list of what a woman does. Check which ones are still valid today.

A real woman—

1. stays in the home with her family where she belongs.
2. makes her children's clothes.
3. irons the sheets each week.
4. never thinks of her own happiness.
5. sacrifices for her children with no thought to her own development.
6. never does things just for herself.
7. doesn't ever let her husband know of her own needs.
8. always gets married.
9. darns her family's socks.
10. cans fruits and vegetables every summer.
11. would never ask her husband to fix dinner.
12. does not seek to develop her own talents. She must always be concerned about others.
13. must never earn more than her husband earns.

14. considers her talents as important to God as any man's talents.
15. considers it wise to develop marketable skills.
16. always makes time for every request made of her.
17. always speaks politely in soft tones.
18. feels guilty either for what she's not doing in the home or for what she's not doing professionally.
19. realizes that Heavenly Father will answer her prayers about her role in life.

How did you do? For the list of men, I checked numbers four, fifteen, and nineteen as still being valid today. For list for women, I checked numbers fourteen, fifteen, and nineteen.

Just as Sam remembered his mother making gingerbread cookies, we also remember our own parents and the things they did.

My father could fix anything that went wrong in the house. He serviced his own car. He did minor plumbing in the home. In all the years I was growing up, we never had a repairman come to our home. My dad did it all.

After I was married, I tried to follow in my dad's footsteps. It was a disaster. Once I tried to fix a leaky faucet and ended up having to replace the entire faucet. It cost me sixty dollars for what should have cost a dime.

And so what did I do? I did what any reasonable person would do. I felt guilty and inadequate. A real man should be able to repair a faucet, but I couldn't. I felt my very manhood was on the line.

Finally I said to myself: "Hey, why should I feel guilty just because I don't have the same talents my father had? There's things I can do that he couldn't. He and I are different. Why should I judge myself on what his talents and abilities were? Why not do what I do best?"

After that, we hired people to fix our leaky faucets. But isn't that a copout? Isn't the very message of this book that we can do anything we want to do?

Yes, but I don't want to do minor plumbing!

There, I've said it. Gee, I feel a lot better now. What I most want to do with my extra time now is write. And so let me do what I do best and let the plumber do what he or she does best. If my plumber needs me to write a sentence, I'll be happy to do it (especially if I can charge what plumbers charge).

Women in the church are subject to feelings of guilt. Just because your mother made bread doesn't mean you have to. Just because your mother ironed sheets doesn't mean you have to. Just because your mother made apple pies from scratch doesn't mean you have to.

We all need the ability to sluff off outdated "shoulds." The kind that say a woman should do this and a man should do that.

In the March 1986 issue of the *Ensign*, the following question was asked of Barbara W. Winder, Relief Society general president: "Some women who must work battle with feelings of guilt as well as the disapproval of some ward members and leaders. How can these women cope with these feelings?"

This was her answer. "I think they will not feel guilty if they will counsel with Heavenly Father in making the decision. If the decision is right, they will feel at peace. That is the key. If they have made the wrong decision, they will tend to feel troubled."

"It is important for us to remember that what others are doing may be what is best for them. For every person, there is a different set of circumstances. Each of us can receive revelation for our own individual needs and responsibilities. We must take strength in that knowledge and live to be worthy of that blessing."

Sister Winder was next asked: "On the other hand, some women who are full-time homemakers feel unhappy and unfulfilled, as if they could be doing something to develop their potential. How can they cope with these feelings?"

She answered: "First, they need to realize that, in teaching and training their children, they are fulfilling the Lord's commandments. And women *can* develop themselves at home. Raising a family requires a great many different skills, each of which can be learned through the experiences we have in our homes.

"I think a lot depends on a woman's attitude. I have met many women who have chosen to stay at home and who are doing wonderful things with their families and making worthwhile contributions in their communities. They do not feel bored or put down because they are staying at home. They know they are developing in those areas most closely related to their eternal potential.

"Whatever a woman feels inspired to do with her life, she should feel at peace and enjoy it! We need to enjoy the good things we are doing!"

Here's what President Gordon B. Hinckley said: "I am grateful that women today are afforded the opportunity to study for science, for the professions, and for every other facet of human knowledge. You are as entitled as are men to the Spirit of Christ, which enlightens every man and woman who comes into the world. (See D&C 84:46.) Set your priorities in terms of marriage and family, but also pursue educational programs which will lead to satisfying work and productive employment in case you do not marry, or to a sense of security and fulfillment in the event you do marry.

"It's also important to enhance one's appreciation of the arts and culture, which are of the very substance of our civilization. Can anyone doubt that good music is godly or that there can be something of the essence of heaven in great art? Education will increase your appreciation and refine your talent."

In a marriage it is important to face the excess baggage each partner brings to the marriage. This consists of certain assumptions of what our marriage will be, such as "When I'm sick my wife should drop whatever she's doing and bring me homemade soup in bed," or "My husband should be a wonderful gardener like my father."

In *Sam*, Lara and Sam eventually begin to communicate more openly about the expectations they each have for their marriage.

We begin with Lara speaking.

"Last night I decided I don't want to run competition with you. When you leave for work in the morning, I want you to know you have a little bit of heaven waiting for you when you come home."

"Why should you be the one to do all the changing?" I asked. "I can learn to adjust to your working."

"I want to quit my job."

"You're just surrendering?"

"It's not a war, Sam. Why can't I have the freedom to change my priorities? I want to spend more time with Adam and I want some children of my own. Maybe after our children are grown, I'll go back to work."

"Grown? They haven't even been conceived yet."

She smiled coyly. "I'm sure we can work that out."

"But if you quit," I said, suddenly worried, "what'll we do for food and rent?"

"My man'll provide for our needs," she said, full of confidence.

"Me?" I croaked.

"Hey, where's all that Self-Knowledge? I saw you in the desert, killing our supper with only a song and a rock,

*starting a fire without matches, saving me from a rattle-
snake. You can do anything you want."*

"You believe that?"

"Sure, you're terrific. Cute, too."

"But you'd just quit your job?" I asked weakly.

*"Sam, why are we arguing? Yesterday you asked me to
quit working. Today I say I will. Now you're trying to talk
me out of it." . . .*

*"Are we ever going to figure this out?" I asked. "Let's
start with the basics. You're a woman and I'm a man."*

"Nice combination, don't you think?"

"And you're my wife."

"Considering the past few months, I'd better be."

"And I'm your husband."

"So far it all ties together quite logically, doesn't it?"

*"In olden times, I'd rule and reign over you. But those
days are gone forever. So what do I do?"*

*"You preside, Sam. You're the president of our family,
and I'm your vice-president. . . . Why don't I stay home
with Adam and make gingerbread cookies and have some
children?"*

"You'd make gingerbread cookies?" I wavered.

"Dozens and dozens."

*"Oh, I don't know, Lara," I moaned. "You've got what it
takes to be a big success in business. I don't want to deny
you any opportunities. . . . Lara, I don't need gingerbread
cookies anymore. What I need is help with my business.
The computer business is one of the fastest growing industries in America, but I'm losing my shirt. You're the genius
at marketing. I need your help."*

*She sighed. "You'll never know how good that sounds to
me."*

The fact that Lara decided to quit her job is not as
significant as the fact that the two of them talked it out

and came to a mutual decision. It fits their particular situation.

Remember that we have been counseled by the Lord not to run faster than we have strength. (See Mosiah 4:27.) He wants us to order our priorities.

Because of such rapid changes in our society each of us faces similar decisions about what to do with our lives. Each decision is unique. We should spend time considering the various choices in our lives.

We should study it out in our minds, study and plan, reach a tentative decision, and then approach Heavenly Father with what we've come up with.

And once we embark on our journey, we should not let Our Bad News Coach tell us that we've made the wrong choice.

There is nobody as interested in our development and progress as Heavenly Father. Isn't it nice that we can go to him and ask his advice and that he will answer our prayers?

And that is the subject of the next chapter.

Homework

Spend time thinking about what your expectations of marriage are. Decide which of these can be sluffed off and which are absolutely necessary. How will you help your spouse make these important decisions?

CHAPTER ELEVEN

If You Need Anything,
Just Ask

A few years ago I agreed to be a priesthood adviser for twenty-four hours at a stake girls' camp. At that time, girls' camp was held in the woods with no buildings nearby.

On the day I drove to the camp, it had been raining since early morning. Thick dark clouds, barely moving at all, blanketed the sky.

I arrived and met with the camp director. She told me that a testimony meeting for the girls was scheduled that night. The problem was that there was no place to have the meeting. She and I walked from tent to tent, trying to figure out how to cram sixty girls in a five-man tent.

We entered one of the tents and found four girls kneeling on their sleeping bags. "Come in," one of them said cheerfully, "we're just about to say a prayer."

We knelt down with the girls. We could hear the steady dripping of the rain on the roof of the tent.

One of the girls asked me if I'd offer the prayer.

"Sure, what are we praying for?" I asked.

"We're praying for the rain to stop," the girl replied.

Oh no, I thought. There's no way the rain's going to stop. These clouds go for fifty miles in every direction and there's no wind to blow them away.

I looked at the girls' faces. They actually believed that God was going to stop the rain for them.

What am I going to do? I thought. There's no way the rain's going to stop. We'll pray, and it'll keep on raining, and that'll shatter the faith of these girls.

Then I thought of a plan. I would offer such a wishy-washy prayer that I wouldn't really ask for anything, and that would leave Heavenly Father a way to get out of this mess.

And so I began a "nonprayer." First I told Heavenly Father that although we might personally like it to stop raining, we must always keep in mind that agriculture is the number one industry in South Dakota, and although we might personally like it to stop raining, the farmers around here need the rain. And far be it from us to deny them moisture.

It was agony for me. I tried to word it so that it sort of sounded like a prayer, but I never actually came out and asked God to do anything.

Just from the mental effort of trying to word it right, I could feel the sweat pouring down my face. As I mumbled on and on, we could hear the rain hitting the roof of the tent.

After a couple of minutes I finished. And when I did, I noticed there was no sound of rain on the tent. I went outside, looked up, and stuck out my hand. The clouds looked exactly as they had all day. And yet it wasn't raining.

I thought to myself, "Well, this won't last."

But it did. The girls had their testimony meeting that night. The clouds had a doughnut-hole opening so we could see stars directly overhead but not anywhere else. Amazingly, the farmers got the rain they needed, and we received what we needed.

After the testimony meeting, we returned to our tents

and got ready for bed. A few minutes later the clouds filled in the opening above us and it started to rain again.

It was a miracle, and every person there knew it.

Why did Heavenly Father perform a miracle for us? Certainly not because of me. I had no confidence at all that he would stop the rain just because a bunch of girls asked him to.

Then why did he do it?

I've thought about that a lot. I think he did it because he loved those girls, and also because they had unquestioning faith in him.

Whoever you are, wherever you live, whatever your place in life, God loves you just as much as he loved those girls. He knows you by name. He thinks about you. You're his son or daughter, and when you lived with him before coming to earth, he cherished you.

And now that you're here on earth, he misses you; he worries about you. Like any parent with a son or daughter away, he wants the very best for you.

You know, he'd like to hear from you once in a while. Just to let him know how things are going. Oh sure, he can always look down and see, but it'd be nice to hear it from your own lips.

Find a time when you're all alone, then kneel down and talk to him. Say the words out loud. Talk to him. Tell him how school is going, tell him about your accident. Tell him how you're getting along with your parents. If you've done something wrong, tell him about it, and ask him to help you to repent. Tell him what's troubling you. If you don't like to go to church, tell him. If you hate algebra, tell him. If you wish you didn't have to go to seminary, tell him. If you wish you could live more like your nonmember friends, let him know about it. If you're lonely, tell him.

He cares about you. He's never too busy for you. He

doesn't mind if you keep coming back to him again and again. He wants to help out. So let him know what you need.

Listen to what Jesus said: "Therefore ye must always pray unto the Father in my name; and whatsoever ye shall ask the Father in my name, which is right, believing that ye shall receive, behold it shall be given unto you." (3 Nephi 18:19-20.)

I used to think that God was too busy to be bothered everytime I lost my keys or forgot where I put my wallet. But listen to this: "Ye are commanded in all things to ask of God, who giveth liberally." (D&C 46:7.)

It says that in all things we can ask God. We can ask for help when we lose our keys. We can ask him to help when we have an exam. We can ask him to help us get some friends when we move to a new town. We can ask for help when we're learning a foreign language. We can ask him when we're trying to lose weight. We can ask him when we're trying to repent of past mistakes.

If it's important to us, we can ask God for help, because he is our Father in Heaven and he loves us dearly.

So go ahead and ask.

How will Heavenly Father answer your prayers? He has many ways. Sometimes he answers prayer through the actions of others. If you are praying for the answer to a question, it might be good to listen very carefully to the talks in sacrament meeting or to your teachers in church. Maybe he'll provide you with a home teacher or bishop who can help.

He may answer your question through an article in the *New Era* or the *Ensign*. Your question may be answered in the form of advice from your parents. You may get your answer from reading the scriptures. He may answer it by giving you thoughts that provide the answer. He may even strengthen you so you can endure your situation better.

He has many ways to help, but one thing I'm sure of, he will answer you.

Homework

Find some time this week when you can be alone and can talk to Heavenly Father. Actually say the words, don't just think them.

He likes for you to keep in touch.

God is more interested in your future than you are, and that's a fact. Please go to him in prayer.

CHAPTER TWELVE

Wrapping It Up

"So what's the point of it all?" my Bad News Coach asks as I shuffle through the growing pile of pages that will eventually make up this book.

It's a fair question. Let me try to come up with some answers. The following things are what I hope you'll have gained from your experience with this book:

1. A feeling that you have many undiscovered talents that you brought from your premortal life.

2. A willingness to try a variety of activities just to see which ones you like the most.

3. A realization that you need to get rid of outdated negative labels about yourself.

4. Encouragement that it's important for you to have positive images in your mind about your future.

5. A knowledge of how to repent so your past doesn't cripple your future.

6. Experience with goal setting so you can turn any ambiguous hope into a day-by-day set of steps that will lead to the accomplishment of the goal.

7. An understanding of some common misconceptions about perfection.

8. The need we have to admit that none of us are Superman or Wonder Woman. We can't do everything.

9. The desire to make God a partner in life through prayer.

The world is full of self-improvement books. And they do remarkably well. This generation seems so concerned with "self" that it is sometimes called the "Me Generation."

Of course God does want you to become self-confident, talented, and successful. But along with that you need to understand something that you can't get from the world's version of self-improvement. *God wants to bless the world through you.* The scriptures indicate that through Abraham's seed all the kindreds of the earth would be blessed. (See 1 Nephi 15:18, D&C 124:58.) A faithful member of the Church becomes of the seed of Abraham. (D&C 84:34.) Because of this, a part of your mission in life is to bless the lives of those around you.

Let's consider an example where someone who developed his talents was able to work in partnership with God to bless the lives of many. Picture in your mind David as a boy, before he met Goliath, when he was first put in charge of his father's flocks.

At first, David thinks they're just a bunch of dumb sheep. He does his job only because he knows he'll get in trouble with his father if he doesn't.

One day while tending sheep, he makes himself a sling and does some target practice. "I bet I can hit that big boulder over there," he thinks. So he whirls the leather strap and lets the stone go. Whap! He misses.

But he keeps practicing, and gradually he gets so he can hit anything he aims at. It becomes automatic to him. Of course there's no thought that he's doing this for the glory of God. He's doing it mainly because he's bored out there with nothing but sheep for company.

At night around the campfire, David doesn't have

much to do, so he decides to learn how to play the guitar (called a harp in those days). Sometimes he makes up his own songs. At first he isn't very good, but the sheep don't seem to mind, so he keeps practicing.

As time goes on, he becomes a good musician. He's developing his talents just for fun, just to give him something to do.

As the days slip by, he finds himself developing a big-brother kind of feeling for the sheep. He realizes that their very survival depends on his ability to find them food and water and to protect them.

One day a lion comes and tries to drag away one of the sheep. Perhaps a hired hand would have just let the lion go. After all, what difference does one sheep make when you've got a whole flock of them. But over the weeks, David has become a shepherd—he loves his flock. He can't stand to see even one of them hurt, so he takes out after the lion, and eventually, after a fierce battle, he kills it.

Later a bear comes. Because David has already killed a lion, he's confident he can kill the bear. And he does.

Because of the lion and the bear, David has confidence in himself.

One day his father asks him to take some food to his brothers in the army. While there, he hears Goliath insult the God of Israel and challenge someone to come fight him.

David volunteers to fight Goliath. The king tells him he's too young. But David says, "Thy servant kept his father's sheep, and there came a lion, and a bear, and took a lamb out of the flock: and I went out after him, and smote him, and delivered it out of his mouth: and when he arose against me, I caught him by his beard, and smote him, and slew him. Thy servant slew both the lion and the bear: and this uncircumcized Philistine shall be as one of them, seeing he hath defied the armies of the living

God. . . . The LORD that delivered me out of the paw of the lion, and out of the paw of the bear, he will deliver me out of the hand of this Philistine." (1 Samuel 17:34-37.)

And so what started as flinging stones at boulders led to killing a lion and a bear. Without those early experiences, David would never have dared to go out and face Goliath. He went out to face Goliath with no armor, no shield, and no sword. Why? Because he'd never practiced using a sword. He went out there with what he had confidence in, a sling and five smooth stones.

Because he had learned how to fling a stone with great accuracy, David killed Goliath and put the entire army of the Philistines into retreat.

From David's talent for making up songs comes the Psalms of David. Listen to the majesty of just one of David's psalms: "The Lord is my shepherd; I shall not want. He maketh me to lie down in green pastures: he leadeth me beside the still waters. He restoreth my soul: he leadeth me in the paths of righteousness for his names' sake. Yea, though I walk through the valley of the shadow of death, I will fear no evil: for thou art with me; thy rod and thy staff they comfort me. Thou preparest a table before me in the presence of mine enemies: thou anointest my head with oil; my cup runneth over. Surely goodness and mercy shall follow me all the days of my life: and I will dwell in the house of the Lord forever." (Psalm 23.)

Only a shepherd who loved his flock could have written that.

How many lives have been blessed by these words? Literally millions. And yet it all began with a boy tending a flock of sheep.

God used David's talents, and he can use yours too.

Finally here's the one last crucial thing that needs to be said before we part company: *Happiness comes when we serve others.*

"Behold, I tell you these things that ye may learn wisdom, that ye may learn that when ye are in the service of your fellow beings ye are only in the service of your God." (Mosiah 2:17.)

In Mosiah 18:7-9, Alma outlines the responsibilities of being members of the church: "And now, as ye are desirous to come into the fold of God, and to be called his people, and are willing to bear one another's burdens, that they may be light: Yea, and are willing to mourn with those that mourn; yea, and comfort those that stand in need of comfort, and to stand as witnesses of God at all times and in all places that ye may be in, even until death, that ye may be redeemed of God, and be numbered with those of the first resurrection, that ye may have eternal life."

You can use every talent you develop to uplift those around you.

Homework

1. Let's begin in church among your own age group. Sometimes young people will form a tightly knit clique and will keep out those even in the same age group. Is there anyone in your age group who is not welcomed at church activities? What can you do to make someone who's lonely feel part of your group?

2. What about in school? Who do your friends make fun of? Who among you is ignored or ridiculed. Show some kindness to that person.

I once wrote a story called "The Least of These, My Brother." In it, Ernie, the one in school everybody makes fun of, decides to join the church. He talks to Jed, a member of the church who has done everything he could to discourage Ernie about the church.

"I guess you're upset about my joining the church, aren't you?"

"No," Jed said. "The Church is for everyone."

"But you'd like to choose which of those everyones joins, wouldn't you? A rich man, or a beautiful girl, an athlete, a talented artist, an influential politician. I'm not any of those things, am I? Do you think there's room in your church for me?"

Jed felt as if he'd been hit.

Ernie continued. "For the first time in my life, I now have a reason to live. But you've always had that, haven't you? It was very comfortable, wasn't it? Having the truth while the rest of us stumbled around in the dark. I'd like to know how you feel, Jed. Not that it matters, I guess, because I'm going to be baptized. Not because of your example, but in spite of it."

Jed walked away. His face felt as if it were on fire.

This causes Jed to change his mind about spending the weekend with the family of the most beautiful girl in school; instead he decides to attend Ernie's baptism. The girl is furious with him. He tries to tell her what he's learned. He says, *"Nobody's a born loser. We make the losers, you and me, by the way we treat them. We carefully mold them each day of their lives. But to the Savior, nobody's a loser."*

She shook her head, turned away, and walked quickly down the hall.

I too have been blessed by the kindness of friends. When I was in high school, my mother came down with rheumatoid arthritis. As the months dragged by, she became progressively weaker, her fingers became more deformed, and her ability to walk quickly faded away.

I graduated from high school and went to college. At Christmas break I came home again. Seeing my mother for the first time in months, it was obvious to me how much worse she had become.

My dad asked me to stay home during the days and

take care of my mom. The woman who had been caring for her needed to be with her own family over Christmas vacation.

Each day of the vacation seemed much like the one before. When my mother awoke, I would lift her out of bed into the wheelchair. I helped her wash by getting the washcloth wet with warm water, putting soap on it, and handing it to her. When she was finished, I would rinse it out, help her get the soap off, and help her with the towel. Eventually we got to the kitchen, and I fixed her something to eat. After breakfast I'd get her some aspirin and a Darvon. Then I wheeled her into the living room and turned on the TV. It didn't matter what was on. Just anything to take her mind off the pain. About eleven o'clock the mail came. At noon I fixed her lunch. In the afternoon she tried to walk. I'd stand beside her and hold onto her, and she'd put one foot a couple of inches in front of the other and slowly move forward. After going a couple of feet she'd be exhausted, and I would put her on the couch so she could rest.

One day she wanted us to make Christmas cookies for my dad. I was in a particularly bleak mood that day but agreed to go ahead.

I started on the recipe, adding each ingredient as it was listed. "A cup of sugar," I read, going to the cupboard.

"That's not enough."

"It says one cup," I grumbled.

"I usually change the recipe. I put in more sugar."

"How much more?"

"Just a little more."

"A cup more, a teaspoon more, what is it!" I snapped.

Eventually we got over that crisis.

After I finished mixing the cookie dough, I put down some waxed paper on the table and rolled out the dough.

My mother wanted to help with the cookies to please my dad. I gave her one of the cookie cutters. She took it, balanced it between her two gnarled hands, and tried to push down hard enough to cut out the form—but she couldn't do it. She didn't even have enough strength in her fingers and hands to do even a simple thing like that.

Suddenly tears streamed down her face. I picked up the cookie dough, slammed it in the garbage can, and stormed outside to try to calm down.

Outside in our backyard I silently cursed the very idea of Christmas. I felt anger toward every family who was happy.

A few minutes later I went in, rolled my mother in her wheelchair back into the living room, and turned on the TV. We never talked about what had happened.

Later that day Sister Leckie, a friend of my mother's from Relief Society, came over to give my mother a permanent. I went to a store just to get away for a while.

When I came back, Sister Leckie was standing behind where my mother sat, brushing out her hair, talking a mile a minute. When she was finished, she told my mother how nice she looked.

My mother, hunched over, weighing ninety pounds, smiled. "Well good," she said. "I wouldn't mind being sick if I looked all right."

My mother anxiously waited for my dad to come home so she could show him how nice she looked with her new hairdo. She really seemed happy to have had her hair done.

Later that week, some carolers came from the church to our house and sang Christmas carols. The music filled our house as they sang to us.

I will never forget the effect these two acts of kindness had upon me. It turned the bleakest of days into something very special, a tender experience I will never forget. (Much later I wrote about it in a story called "A Christmas Song.")

The Savior said it best, "Inasmuch as ye have done it unto one of the least of these my brethren, ye have done it unto me." (Matthew 25:40.)

Use the talents God has given you to bless the lives of those around you.

It looks like we've come to the end of this.

I've thought about you a lot lately. I hope you won't mind, but I've imagined the two of us fishing from a boat on a beautiful mountain lake. Occasionally, when there's a lull in the action, we have a chance to talk. I try to explain what life has taught me about you.

To tell you the truth, I'm in awe of your talents. The world will be richly blessed by your having lived in it.

You *can* make a difference. The thoughts you think, the talents you share, the kindness you extend to others, and the allegiance you give to righteousness can make all the difference in the world.

Well, the sun's about to set, and because we're both so very good at fishing, we've got ourselves a nice catch. So let's reel in and call it a day.

So long. Have a nice life.

Sources Cited

Books

Covey, Stephen R. *The Divine Center*. Salt Lake City, Utah: Bookcraft, 1982, p. 54.

Edwards, Betty. *Drawing on the Right Side of Your Brain*. Houghton Mifflin Co., 1979.

Evans, Richard L., Jr. *Richard L. Evans: The Man and the Message*. Salt Lake City, Utah: Bookcraft, 1973.

Fisher, Garth, and Dennis Remington. *How To Lower Your Fat Thermostat*. Vitality House International, 1983.

Lucas, Jerry, and Harry Lorayne. *The Memory Book*. Ballantine, 1975.

Smith, Joseph F. *Gospel Doctrine*. Salt Lake City, Utah: Deseret Book Company, 1975, pp. 93-94; 100-101.

Smith, Joseph Fielding. *Taking Heed to Yourselves!* Salt Lake City, Utah: Deseret Book Company, 1966, p.345.

Articles

Gardner, John G. "Achievement & Eternal Progression." *Ensign*, March 1966, p. 181.

Hinckley, Gordon B. "The Continuing Pursuit of Truth," *Ensign*. April 1986, p. 2.

———. "Ten Gifts from the Lord." *Ensign*, November 1985, p. 89.

Lee, Harold B. "A Sure Trumpet Sound: Quotations from President Lee." *Ensign*, February 1974, p. 78.

————. "Stand Ye in Holy Places." *Ensign*, July 1973, pp. 122-23.

————. "Understanding Who We Are Brings Self-Respect." *Ensign*, January 1974, p. 5.

Owens, Jesse. "1936: Golden Moment of Triumph." *Saturday Evening Post*, Jan/Feb 1976, p. 48.

Reusch, Rebecca. "Eating His Words." *This People*, May 1985, p. 46.

Winder, Barbara W. "Enriching & Protecting the Home." *Ensign*, March 1986, p. 21.

Woodbury, Richard. "One Man's Life of No Regrets." *Life*, March 24, 1972, p. 66-68.

By Jack Weyland

A New Dawn. Salt Lake City, Utah: Deseret Book Company, 1984.

Charly. Salt Lake City, Utah: Deseret Book Company, 1980.

Home Cooking on the Wasatch Range. Play produced at Brigham Young University, Provo, Utah.

Sam. Salt Lake City, Utah: Deseret Book Company, 1981.

"Sometimes a Phone Call." *New Era*, February 1976.

"The Emergence of Butterflies." *New Era*, April 1979, p. 28. Reprinted in *First Day of Forever*. Bountiful, Utah: Horizon, 1980.

"The Least of These, My Brother." *New Era*, November 1976.

Index